Exclusive distributors;

Book Sales Limited
8/9 Frith Street, London, W1V 5TZ, England

The Putnam Publishing Group
200 Madison Avenue, New York, NY10016, USA

Music Sales Pty. Limited,
120 Rothschild Avenue, Rosebery, NSW 2018, Australia

To the Music Trade Only:

Music Sales Limited
120 Rothschild Avenue, Rosebery, NSW 2018, Australia

Music Sales Corporation
225 Park Avenue South, New York, NY10003, USA

Published 1982 by Omnibus Press
(a division of Book Sales Ltd)

Book design by John Gordon
Picture research by Valerie Boyd

This book © copyright 1982 Omnibus Press

All rights reserved. No part of this book may be reproduced in any form or by any electronic or mechanical means, including information storage or retrieval systems, without permission in writing from the publisher, except by a reviewer who may quote brief passages in a review.

ISBN 0-7119-0054-X
UK Order No. OP 41615

Typeset by: Cogent Typesetters Ltd., London

Printed in England by Courier International Limited, Tiptree, Essex

Picture credits: Camera Press 10, 11/Andre Csillag 88 (inset)/Decca Record Company Ltd, 24/David Wedgbury Decca Record Company Ltd, 6, 9, 15, 16/Stevie Dixon 36, 96/E.M.I. 74, 75/Granada Television 95/L.F.I. 3, 27, 39, 54/Elain Bryant L.F.I. 89/(Paul Canty L.F.I. 79(top)/Paul Cox L.F.I. 88/Neil Jones L.F.I. 65/Michael Putland L.F.I. 62, 94/Chris Walter L.F.I. 55, 68, 76/Melody Maker 22, 23, 50/Spud Murphy 34/Barry Plummer front and back cover, 1, 4, 28, 31, 37, 40, 42, 45, 46, 47, 48, 51, 52/53, 56, 64, 66, 69, 70, 71, 72, 73, 79 (bottom), 80, 81, 84/85, 92/David Wainwright Photofeatures 86/Chris Walter Photofeatures 90/Rex Features Int. front cover (inset) 33, 59, 77, 91/Bill Orchard Rex Features 82/Paul Sinclair 13, 18, 21/Stevenson 29.

ELECTRIC WARRIOR
The Marc Bolan Story
Paul Sinclair

Omnibus Press
London/New York/Sydney

For permission to reprint from interviews I acknowledge the following publications; Sounds, Record Mirror, New Musical Express, Melody Maker, Zig Zag, Rolling Stone, Creem and The Evening Standard (London). The interview with Andy Ellison is reprinted by kind permission of Ros Davies and Colin Jackson. The interviews with Herbie Flowers, Keith Altham, George Tremlett, Rosalind Russell, Steve Peregrine Took and Simon Napier-Bell were all conducted by the author. The author sends special thanks for information and help to Andy Ellison and June Bolan. Dedicated to Mike Richards, John Williams, Alan Seterfield, Jean and Rarn Gang (Gwent) and all true fans who still have Marc in their hearts.

Chapter 1

On September 30, 1947, a little boy called Marc was born in Hackney Hospital, London, to Simeon and Phyllis Feld. Phyllis ran a fruit stall in Berwick Street Market, Soho. Simeon, a real Cockney, was a cosmetic salesman during the week while at weekends he sold fancy goods from a stall in Petticoat Lane. Marc had a step-brother called Harry from Simeon's previous marriage.

Phyllis Feld remembers that young Marc was very strong-willed and would kick anyone he didn't like. Even as a toddler he was in a world of his own. He used to believe he was Audie Murphy, then Mighty Joe Young and finally The Phantom of the Opera! As an avid cinema-goer he saw all the science fiction and horror films and could name every title, actor, producer and director.

"The first thing I really remember is going to a big green common. I remember sitting on the front porch at home. I must have been very young. I remember being a toddler in Stoke Newington, which is in London. I seem to remember ten years of my life sitting on the front porch. And we had a big flower-bed. I used to sit on that too. There was always a lot of flooding in our road. We used to go and swim in the water or go upstairs!

"My first school was called Northwood Primary. It was just up the top of our road. It's only a little road . . . in those days it seemed like miles and miles! On my first day at school I got beaten up. On the next two days I got beaten up too. But on the third day I beat up the bloke who kept hitting me. It was all right after that! It was a nice school really. I remember liking playing with rubber bricks and making things with them. I've never seen rubber bricks since. I remember the first lady teacher I had. She used to hang her petticoat up in the classroom. It was quite astonishing now I think of it. She never took it off in front of the kids. She must have taken it off during the break 'cos when we came back from playtime it was there hanging up!

"My first hobbies were the same as most kids . . . we had a gang. We were quite rough. I got knifed when I was a kid. Our gang was called The Sharks, like the guys in West Side Story. I was only eight, mind. We used to rush around the streets. We used to wear our dad's army helmets – the ones they had in the war. I remember liking the gang, being part of it."

When he was eight his parents bought him a drum kit even though Simeon was only making £4.10s a week as a lorry driver. When he was nine they bought him a £16 guitar.

"I loved my childhood – looking back, I wouldn't want to swop it for anyone's. In a way I'd like to be young again – you can tell from my music."

His first attempt to become a serious musician was at the legendary 2 I's a coffee bar in Old Compton Street where he had been helping out behind the counter serving espresso.

"He was too young," recalls Mrs Feld. "I think they only let him do it to keep him happy. But he never let things like that get him down. He just came back, shut himself in his room for a while then came out and said 'Well I've tried that. I'll try something else now!'"

In 1959 while still at school he played tea-chest bass for a three-piece busking band called Susie & The Hula Hoops. The two other members were Stephen Gould on guitar and the young Helen Shapiro who found fame as a child star a few months later. Her sudden rise to fame made a big impact on Marc and at 12 years old he decided to leave school as soon as possible and have a crack at show biz . . .

"I always had trouble at school. I failed my 11-plus. I was really quite good at school, except I was hopeless at maths. I went to a big secondary modern school called the William Wordsworth School – I remember being told on my first day it was named after a famous poet. There was a school up the road called the Daniel Defoe School. It was a riding-school, with horses and things. We used to fight between the schools all the time.

"I always hung around with the rough kids. Perhaps it was because I was in the lowest class. They were sweet kids really. But they were always on their guard. That type's insecure really. They take some time to accept you as one of them. By the time I was in second year I was the best fighter! And nobody would have said different. 'Cos my brother was so much older than the other kids anyway!

"They just wouldn't answer my questions at school. I mean questions about real life things – about the whole business of growing up. I was an okay pupil in Art and History, but I wanted to find out about things that you couldn't just look up in books."

The girls from the 'Oh Boy' TV show used to take him to all their performances at the Hackney Empire. He was always proud to relate how he once carried Eddie Cochran's guitar from the theatre.

In 1960, during the Teddy Boy era, Marc, then 13 years old and wearing black and white two-tone shoes, tight black drainpipes, and an 'Everly Bros.' shirt, sat on his garden wall admiring a passing Teddy Boy. The Ted was followed down the street by Martin Kauffman "and he had on very, very baggy ginger Harris-tweed trousers, a pair of green hand-made shoes with sidebuckles and long points, and a dark green blazer with drop shoulders, one button cut-away, very short. I checked out later where all the stuff came from. The shirt was made by Harry Flash, and was dark green, with a very high-backed collar so one's hair would go over the back. His hair was parted straight down the middle like Hitler's, over both eyes.

"The impact of having just seen what one thought was a real trendy looking Teddy Boy and then seeing this cat . . . I can't trace how he got like that. But I knew something was going on." He followed Kauffman for hours.

He bought a £5 pair of shoes from Stan Bartholomew's and got his mum to buy him a suit from Burton's on hp – made to his own design.

All his money from after-school jobs and the market stall takings was spent on clothes and he became the 'heaviest face' at the local amusement arcade.

"At that time I was only about 12. I found that clothes thing very appealing visually, and I got right in there and made myself look like these other cats who were somewhat older than I was. By the time the Mod thing really happened I was out of it and living in France. I was never a Mod . . . there was no such thing then; that all came later, 'Ready, Steady, Go' and all that sort of stuff. I used to spend all my time round at my friends' houses. We used to drink black coffee and listen to records all day."

Walking down Oxford Street one day he chanced to meet journalist Angus

McGill of the Evening Standard. Marc boasted to him that he owned "10 suits, 8 jackets, 15 pairs of slacks, 30 to 35 good shirts, about 20 jumpers and 3 leather jackets." McGill went home with Marc to see this collection and later included him in a feature about Mods that he was writing for Town magazine.

"I was always a star, even if it was only being the star of three streets in Hackney. Actually I think everybody's a potential star at something. It just depends how strong your ambition is, whether you actually fulfil that potential. I'm not ambitious as such, but there was no way that I was going to be made to do anything I didn't wanna do. I'm all for anyone who's an exhibitionist. You've got to be different."

Pictures for Marc's first appearance in print were taken by ace photographer Don McCullin with fellow models Peter Sugar and Michael Simmonds. "He made us sort of look like convicts. He got very hard looking pictures," said Marc later. Writer Peter Barnsley commented beneath one picture, "Where is the goal towards which he is obviously running as fast as his impeccably shod feet can carry him? It is nowhere. He is running to stay in the same place, and he knows by the time he has reached his mid-twenties the exhausting race will be over and he will have lost."

But young Marc Feld wasn't going to lose. One day he returned to the old amusement arcade. "It was my first encounter with sussing out human nature. I'd been very funky to be around as a face, you know, I was still the heaviest face – the fact that I'd not been around and other cats could move in brought total resentment at having me back there. No one would talk to me and it made me very sad for about five minutes. But I could dig it. It was like I was too heavy. I was in that magazine. All that stuff had come out and I was supposed to be somewhere else. They didn't know where. I'd ascended to Olympus. And suddenly I was there. The funkiest thing I could have done from a theatrical point of view was

split. So I did. It was instant immortality, you see."

A friend in a model agency introduced him to photographic modelling and he became a "John Temple boy". He was also used in the Freemans-type catalogues which Marc's parents still treasure. "At the time, they thought I was very outrageous because I had quite long hair. The flash was that I was in the John Temple shop windows as a cardboard cut-out . . . I didn't much like it. I didn't like the suits – they were terrible and I told them so, actually. But it was worth a grand!"

But at John Temple they remember "he was just another model selected from an agency in our usual twice-yearly search for new faces. But he wasn't an exceptional model. And he was never used again. . ."

Marc and his parents moved to a prefab in Somers Town where Marc used to buy his records from the Treasure Boxshop. "I remember down Tooting Broadway in London there used to be lots of old book shops where you could pick up weird books very cheap. I used to love going there. Everywhere like that used to smell

musty and old. I used to keep my mind on anything but school.

"It was very different from what I'd known before. There were some rough types there and I'd had my picture in a magazine. And because I'd done modelling they called me a right cissy. In the end I stood up for myself and told them all to get lost. Then they realised I was just like them and I made some real friends. Some of them I still see.

"I spent all my time then not going to school. I mean I purposely didn't go." In fact he was expelled at 14 – but he had only a few months to go at school anyway.

After a short lay off from modelling Marc began learning the guitar again. This time he was determined to get into the music business. Having left school he had the time to devote to his new career. Simeon explains, "We honestly didn't mind him being expelled, he just didn't have any interest in school so we encouraged him to go ahead with his music. Whatever he did that music thing was the end of it.

"Marc idolised my Phyllis . . . and she went out and really worked hard so he could stay at home."

And Phyllis says, "We weren't upset when he was expelled because frankly he never went to school very much anyway. And when he did, he went wearing Elvis Presley clothes and winkle-picker shoes which always annoyed them. He was at the same school as his elder brother Harry and they were always asking, 'Why can't you be like him, the good one?'. Marc just said, 'Screw you, don't want to be like him'."

Eventually he got a job to prove he could work. "I used to work in a clothes shop called Edgars in Tooting Broadway and wash up in the Wimpy bar at night. I had two hours sleep at night and I did that for a week and had a mental breakdown – one of those Scott Walker numbers at 16."

"Only jobs he's ever had," commented Phyllis. "I've always said that I was in the same position as mothers whose sons go to college. They have to support them until they are 18 or whatever so I didn't mind supporting Marc while he worked on his songs and that." At 16 Marc decided to try his hand on the folk circuit because he couldn't find anybody else he wanted to play with and also because he only had an old Suzuki Spanish guitar.

Using the name Toby Tyler he played at a few folk clubs. Then an actor called Allan Warren discovered him and became his manager. Their partnership didn't last as long as Bolan's enthusiasm.

Allan Warren recalled, "I used to sing and dance on Rediffusion's pop show 'Five O'Clock Club'. One day I met Toby Tyler who was getting in on the pop scene. I liked him and thought he had a lot of talent. He used to come round to my apartment most nights and play his guitar. Some of my friends used to laugh and say 'not another one trying to make it!'

"I rather saw him as a baby-face copy of Cliff Richard – and frankly that's how Toby styled himself. The idea was that if Toby made it I would manage him." He produced an acetate of Toby singing the Betty Everett number 'You're No Good' for an EMI recording test but they turned him down and Toby and Warren went their separate ways.

Before they split Warren took the young Toby to have some photographs taken by Mike McGrath who remembers: "I took Toby's pictures on the balcony of my Earl's Court flat and outside in the Square. He didn't say a word – Allan Warren did all the talking. When he was there he was like a silent, shy schoolboy."

Marc hung around the actors in the National Theatre and met Riggs O'Hara. They became friends and shared a flat. Marc got the odd part as a delinquent in the Sam Kydd TV series. "I did a lot of character parts like that. But they're so jive all those things, anyway, and I never took acting seriously. I knew I wanted to do something and I knew that wasn't it – I never felt that close to acting. I couldn't see that as something that would really turn me on. It seemed so slow . . .

"I did some kids things. I was in a series called 'Orlando' for instance, but I did all that because I didn't really know what I wanted to do. I was very into sounds then, but I hadn't thought about actually singing, and I did some modelling to get some bread together."

Then Marc got bored and he and Riggs decided to take a trip to France. "I went to France as soon as I left school after my parents had moved from Stamford Hill, Stoke Newington to Wimbledon, and there was nothing there that I could associate with . . . I spent about a year without communication with anyone except my parents and brother. All I used to do was go to the pictures a couple of times a week, the library and second-hand record shops.

"I was in Paris for about six months. . . . I lived in a forest for a while, and then with this cat who was a magician in a château which had about 40 rooms. He was a very powerful, very learned man. I learned a lot of mythology, good things. I read lots of books. He had amazing books there, books by Aleister Crowley and handwritten books and things like that.

"He wasn't a black magician; he had many old books about control of the environment by thought projection, and he could transmit feelings so that you understood what he meant implicitly . . . which is magic to me. It was a Yoga magic rather than one involving sheep sacrifice at midnight on Glastonbury Tor. It was very nice to be around someone like that.

"I learned by watching him for the five months I lived there. And I went on studying magic from books for two years. It's a powerful thing. This man used his magic in the pursuit of knowledge – but black magic is a very selfish thing. It would tend to be dangerous anyway. He could read people's minds and conjure up spirits yet these things were to him normal things.

"I learned a lot in Paris. Rubbed out what school had done. It was there that I decided what I wanted to be. I saw some-

one levitate. He was standing on the floor and he raised himself about eight feet in the air. I've also done magical rites and conjured up demons . . . I've also seen flying saucers. The world is mathematics . . . I mean it's based on maths . . . well there are certain herbs and incantations which can make you invisible. But in fact you don't really become invisible. It's just that you're not visible to the person watching . . . you know, you might not be able to see me, but perhaps you could feel me . . .

"I once conjured up a spirit that wasn't very friendly. It came in the form of a Greek boy. I believe you can do whatever you want to . . . I definitely believe in reincarnation. I believe for a start that all my lyrical ability was learned in a past life as a bard". Marc planned a book for publication called 'Recollections'. "When I read back what I've written it's just like an old man talking – it's just not me – it can't possibly be me. It's centered in a totally alien landscape which I know nothing about. No, there is no way with my background, that one could account for it.

"I wrote out a rite calling to Pan to change me into Satyr. Literally, with hairy legs, hooves and horns. But I realised I couldn't do it. What's going to happen? I'm not going to be able to walk on to an Arcadian hillside and go up to my cave and just hang out. I wouldn't be able to go out of the house for a start. If I did I'd probably get locked up and put in a hospital somewhere and dissected. Or put in a zoo. If Barnum were around he'd put me in a freak show. I'm sure there were Satyrs, in the last hundred years, that were in Barnum's freak shows . . . the rite would've worked. I do know how to do it.

"I want to walk upon the galaxies. I want to hold oceans in my hand. Many people say 'yes, very poetic' – a magician means he wants to hold the oceans in his hand. End of story."

Marc found himself a new manager, in the unlikely guise of 18-year old 'publicist' Mike Purskin. A month before 'The Wizard' was released Marc and Mike Purskin were interviewed and commented on the name change to Bolan. "We thought it looked French at first," Purskin said. "People want to be like Marc: he's leading them somewhere."

"And I don't know where I want to go myself," Marc said. "I was a spoilt child. All I did was tell my mother what was best. I had this thing about Greek gods: the whole idea about centaurs and horses with wings just knocked me out. He returned to the story of his wizard friend: "I met this man who was a black magician and who had a big château on the Left Bank; I only left it about eight times in the year I was there. I learned about the black art, but being evil it didn't basically appeal to me. I think this man was getting old and he wanted to work his magic through me.

"They crucified live cats. Sometimes they used to eat human flesh just like chicken bones. From a cauldron. I don't care whether you believe it or not. It's a bit scary however false it sounds. But what can I do? You tell me. It sounds ego; yet it's true.

"It's really scary: if I go into a room and there are ten girls, nine of them will fancy me. I've never failed with girls yet. I'm sick of modelling and living off wizards. Besides, once I get over the fame, I will know where I stand.

"My ego wouldn't stand dying a death at this moment. I would go right back into my shell and I've only just got out of it after two years. I look forward to growing old, to being mature and knowing good wine, I want to savour life; I want to have grey hair like Cary Grant."

Producer Simon Napier-Bell later commented: "Marc's imagination ran to his biographical details too. The magician he lived with — sometimes it was six months, sometimes it was eighteen months. He met a guy who did conjuring tricks and he spent a weekend with him. I know because he came to me at the time. He was sixteen and a half. He'd spent four weeks in France. It was both true and untrue. His imagination was sparked off and set off in his mind a great fantasy. Sometimes he had a little difficulty remembering which bits were made up and which weren't."

When he came back from Paris Marc increased his emphasis on writing songs. He shut himself away in his room and began "basically to learn the art of writing and playing the guitar." He also worked hard at getting a record contract.

He later recalled he had "been rejected by every record company in the world and thrown out of more office buildings than I care to remember." But eventually he met producer Jim Economedies and signed with Decca. Marc — "They said, 'Kid, with your face, we'll make you a star'." But they didn't.

Marc found he had a new name. When the acetate of 'Wizard' arrived it had 'Marc Bowland' on the white label. He consulted Decca and when the record was eventually released in November 1965 the name had been changed to Marc Bolan.

The Decca press release was a masterpiece of sixties hyperbole:

"Marc Bolan was born in September 1947. After 15 years had passed he travelled to Paris and met a black magician called The Wizard. He lived for 18 months in The Wizard's château with Achimedies, an owl, and the biggest, whitest Siamese cat you ever saw.

He then felt the need to spend some time alone so made his way to woods, near Rome. For two weeks he strove to find himself and then he returned to London where he began to write. His writings mirror his experiences with mentionings of the magician's pact with the great god Pan. In London, walking down Kings Road, Chelsea in the dead of night, he chanced to meet a girl named Lo-og who gave him a magic cat. This cat, named after the girl, is now his constant companion and is a source of inspiration to him.

Now The Wizard's tale is set down for all to hear on Marc's first recording for Decca."

A small poem accompanied two photographs of a very French-looking Bolan.

"Standing alone in the wood,
with the golden palace
bleeding scarlet tears into
the sunset, I thought of all
the treasures in the magic
palace. And all the emptiness
in my stomach and I smiled
secretly, Rememberin' the
wizard's words."

Actually the black cat Lo-og was named after Stones' producer Andrew Loog Oldham and it stayed with Marc's parents until 1972.

Disc reviewed 'The Wizard' as follows: "On the strength of this strange young man's looks and weird background I suspect we'll hear more of this odd record about meeting a Wizard in the woods who knew all. I prefer the other side, 'Beyond the Risin' Sun' which has more tune. Jim Economedies, ace producer, does lovely things on this. I'm a bit put off by the way this boy sings with Dylan phrasing but that's all."

George Melly wrote in the Observer that Bolan was to be likened to Walter De La Mare, the fantasy poet.

Marc found that the magic record contract did not mean instant success. He found himself hustling for interviews and write-ups. One of his first contacts as

Marc Bolan was Evening Standard journalist Angus McGill. "I must say I simply did not recognise him," said McGill later. "I had remembered him as a rather plain little chap and suddenly there was the most glamorous young man you'd ever seen, all curls and exotic clothes. He played the record, which I thought was appalling and showed me a sheaf of poetry which struck me as unmitigated rubbish. But he had determination and such an extraordinary personality that in the end I think I did write a column about him on the lines of working-class lad-trying-to-make-the-big-time. I never thought he'd make it though. But then I once predicted that TV would never catch on either."

Marc performed 'The Wizard' on 'Ready, Steady, Go'. The band missed out the intro, played too fast and in the wrong key. Mr and Mrs Feld also remember the screen going blank for most of Marc's TV début. It was a disaster.

At this point he met journalist Keith Altham who eight years later became his publicist.

Keith: "I knew him as a journalist when I was on the New Musical Express and we used to frequent a bar called The Brewmaster, in Leicester Square. It was around 1965 and he was about 18, 'The Mod about Town', when he used to do modelling, about the time he had his contract with Decca. He came in with a single 'The Wizard' and he used to try and brag to us and say 'Gotta listen to this, fellas, I'm going to be the greatest thing since Elvis Presley', and we thought 'nice little bloke, Marc! Sit down and have a Coka Cola'. He was the kind of hustling figure one never really expected to do the amazing things he later did. I liked him.

"He never had a strong voice so I suppose he made a virtue out of an idiosyncrasy that was there in his voice like most singers do.

"If I think about him as a person – I think there was something special about him, you see somebody like that who is a pushy little guy as he was, yes, there was something special about him but you're not certain, as the years go by, whether you actually knew it at the time or whether you are thinking of it in retrospect. There were some strange things about Marc.

"He was a sort of precocious talent – a sort of boy/man thing, because he lacked a formal education. I've met other people who are artistic but not formally artistic . . . it's an innocence, a kind of naïvete that children have and that we lose as we grow up. There was this very young childlike quality about him, the way that children see colours better than we do, their sense of smell is better and their reactions to certain things are faster. The inability to put things down in grammatical sequence you could see in his writing . . . dyslexic almost . . . was a part of that. He was reacting in the very honest, unaffected way that children do to emotional situations.

"I don't think he traded on it, or even that he was aware he possessed it. It probably gained him other qualities as well that he wasn't aware of. He tended to think that they were almost super-normal talents.

"He put quasi-mystical interpretations on them. I think it was much simpler than

that. He was intuitively right about whether somebody was good, bad or whatever. He wouldn't be able to tell you why or explain the logic behind it."

In June 1966 Decca released 'The Third Degree' backed by what Marc claimed was an unfinished demo – 'San Francisco Poet'. It did nothing. In 1972 Track tried to release 'Jasper C. Debussy' which was intended as the follow-up to 'Third Degree' but by then Marc had moved to Columbia and had changed to producer Simon Napier-Bell, whom he met in late 1966.

Simon Napier-Bell: "Marc 'phoned me in 1966 and came to my flat to play me his songs. He sat in a chair and played them on an acoustic guitar. He had about four albums worth. He was on a very high ego trip at the time. He really didn't think he needed to make records. He thought if we just put some posters up then people would see his photograph and he'd just happen. And I said 'no' I thought a record would be a good idea. So he said it's just me and the guitar.

"He'd done that one record with Decca. He was pre-running what he later did when he left John's Children and went to acoustic. But I thought it wasn't a very good idea but 'if that's what he wanted to do we'll have a try' and I loved all the songs. So we recorded all the songs with just him and the guitar. It's that material which is on the album released by Cherry Red. Then when it was finished he again said, 'Well that's it, now I've done an album it's really going to happen'. He was really ridiculously egotistical to the point where you were furious with him, but he was so totally charming that you had to accept it as probably true. I eventually persuaded him that you had to do something more to the songs, so we decided on 'Hippy Gumbo' which we took and did with some strings. I took it to every record company – and you must remember there were only five record companies then and if anyone was in a position to do anything with it I was. Nobody liked it. So finally I went back and told him and he was completely shattered. He wasn't even expecting to be turned down now, he was absolutely certain of himself. But I didn't lose faith in him. He lost more faith in himself than I did in him."

When 'Hippy Gumbo' came out, backed by 'Misfit', it didn't create as much initial interest as 'The Wizard' but it was a forecast of things to come. It was acoustic with a string quartet overdubbed twice to give it what Brian Sommerville, Marc's then publicist described as a 'powerful atmosphere'. He added "bayou fog seems to creep out of the phonograph as you play it. The combination of simplicity and sophistication is rather reminiscent of 'Porgy and Bess'.

"It features guitar, strings, kettle drums and Marc singing in a voice that is as creole as Gumbo itself. Just how and why Marc wrote a creole song is a mystery, but it may have something to do with his French background. For although Marc was born in London, both his parents are French and he lived in France as a child. However, Marc himself says, I was very Cockney as a kid – French Cockney. Eventually Marc and his family moved back to England but when he was 14 Marc left home and went to Paris. After 18 months there, he moved on to Italy and then to Germany where he acted in films. Marc likes £9,000 cars, Marc dislikes £8,000 cars. Taste in music, rock'n'roll and Chet Baker. 'I've never heard Chet Baker but he looks great. I have all his album covers'." The handout was so inaccurate that it must have even confused Marc!

Marc made another appearance on 'Ready, Steady, Go', this time to promote 'Hippy Gumbo' and to make up for the fiasco of his last appearance. He is still remembered for this performance but it was overshadowed by the first British TV appearance of Jimi Hendrix. Marc later boasted that Hendrix said how much he liked his voice and told Marc he'd never make it!

Chapter 2

Despite the critical acclaim for 'Hippy Gumbo', it was not a chart success and Marc grew restless. Simon Napier-Bell had two other groups on his books. One was The Yardbirds, who at that time included Jimmy Page. Napier-Bell would sometimes let Marc sit in on their sessions. The other group was John's Children who were signed to The Who's label, Track. Marc laid down some solo acoustic tracks for Track after recording 'Hippy Gumbo' and before joining John's Children as their lead guitarist, backing vocalist, main writer and 'creative person'. These solo acoustic demos were later released with John's Children and Tyrannosaurus Rex demos on the Track compilation album 'Beginning of Doves'.

In the last half of 1966, John's Children were becoming an underground flower-power band. Previously they had been a Mod band called The Silence which had developed from a number of ragged hybrids: The Clockwork Onions (Chris Townsen, Andy Ellison, Chris Dawsett, and Geoff McClelland) and The Few (same line-up plus John Hewlett). Their drummer, Chris Townsen, sometimes deputised for Keith Moon.

John Hewlett, now a successful record producer, recalled how Marc Bolan joined his first group. "At first we were called The Silence, and this guy called Geoff McClelland played lead guitar. Marc Bolan joined when we kicked this other bloke out. There was also an organist. He was the only real musician in the group. He left after we changed the name. Simon (Napier-Bell) kind of liked me so we thought we should call it John's Children. We wanted something kind of young."

After the name change, but before Bolan joined, John's Children released two singles – 'The Love I Thought I'd Found' which was a hit in America as, 'Smashed!! Blocked!!' and 'Just What You Want, Just What You'll Get' which flopped. They intended to release a third 'Not The Sort Of Girl (You Take To Bed)' but it was shelved when McClelland left and Bolan joined.

After 'Hippy Gumbo' failed Simon Napier-Bell decided that it would be a good idea for Marc to join John's Children: "I said I thought it was a good idea if he worked towards where he wanted to go by joining John's Children. He would be in a group, he'd make some contacts and some of their fans would become his fans. He could play lead guitar. I wanted to get him back into the idea of rock, his songs were so obviously rock. It worked very well. It restored his ego enough that he wanted to leave them. But that was good."

Hewlett again: "Marc had done a couple of singles like 'Hippy Gumbo' but he hadn't really worked, he was floundering. He wanted to be in a band but he also wanted to be a poet. I had the strongest personality in the band, but Marc had all the good songs. Chris played drums, and Andy sang, but Marc and I were the front guys in the group."

In 1967, in one of the few interviews John's Children ever gave, Marc described their stage act: "We don't just do a musical performance . . . it's a 45 minute happening . . . sometimes we're barely conscious of what we're doing. It's like a big turn-on seance between us and the audience. I've seen Andy go quite mad like a witch doctor in the tribal dance. He leaps off the stage and runs around the audience or sometimes he attacks one of us. In Düsseldorf he got in a fight with John and they both fell 15 feet off the stage on to Andy's head."

In the same interview, Chris Townsen was asked about their growing success. "The reason we're succeeding is 'cos we do everything for ourselves . . . We don't sit around waiting for publicity people to do all our promotional work for us. Yeah, and the money we make from playing we invest in other things. We've got our own club in Leatherhead and a big old house in the country which we're converting into a sort of group home. We're building a swimming pool and we've got a lot of blokes who look after us . . . and they come round to gigs with us on their motor bikes . . . act as an escort and make sure we get our money all right.

"Andy's the lead singer and he jumps off the stage and does somersaults and belts John when he feels like it. He's got a gong to hit as well. And Marc, he usually sits in a trance in the middle of the stage, except when he's jumping about like a flea."

"Bunny" interrupted John. "Kit Lambert says we should have been called The Electric Bunnies."

Then Chris was asked what he did. "Oh, I just play the drums." "Just play the drums?" echoed Andy, "How can he say that? He's the best pop drummer ever, he's sensational, he's fantastic."

And John Hewlett? "Oh, he's the best seducer ever," said Chris, "if we want something from someone and everything else has failed, we send John along. He won't tell us what he does but it always works. It's his eyes I think."

"People who see us play often think we're out of our heads," commented John. "It's true," Andy confirmed, "from the minute we get on stage we lose our minds completely, it's like we're all in a trance." "Marc's songs are part of it", John explained, "they're super dimensitive (sic) . . . not just double meanings but millions of meanings. Take 'Desdemona'. A lot of people say that 'lift up your skirt and speak' is dirty, but it's not. Marc wrote those words because they gave him buzz . . . they weren't meant to mean anything."

Marc and the band emerged after one week in the recording studio with several unfinished backing tracks, demos and releasable tracks, among them 'Desdemona'.

'Desdemona' (written by Marc) was backed with a Hewlett/Townsen song 'Remember Thomas A Beckett'. It reached the lower half of the charts in June 1967 and could have been number one but it was banned by the BBC for the line "lift up your skirts and fly".

A second single was planned with Marc Bolan compositions – 'Midsummer Nights Scene'/'Sarah Crazy Child'. The single was pressed but not released, which displeased Marc. Instead a Hewlett/Townsen song 'Come And Play With Me In The Garden' was chosen and 'Sarah Crazy Child' was tucked away on the flip side. 'Come And Play' was the same backing track as 'Remember Thomas A Beckett' slightly amended and with alternative lyrics.

By now Marc could see he wasn't going to get the control he wanted and needed if he was to be creative and happy. So he split, having been with the group for only three months. After he left, John's Children released 'Go Go Girl' – a Bolan song, with Marc on the backing track but with the words changed. Again a Hewlett/Townsen song was the B-side – 'Jagged Time Lapse'.

John's Children split up a little while after Bolan left but it is still fondly remembered as a distinctive, and in retrospect, legendary band. It was the lift-off point for Bolan and Andy Ellison. Ellison, after several abortive groups (of which Jook was the most notable), re-entered the charts in 1977 as a member of Radio Stars.

In 1977, Andy Ellison was asked about his days with John's Children: "Marc was signed to Simon Napier-Bell. He was a folk artist at the time and he got out a record called 'The Wizard'. We were also signed to Napier-Bell. We chucked out Geoff McClelland because he wasn't very good (he's a bathroom salesman now), and took on Marc, which was the first time he'd ever played electric guitar. I think he was with us for about six months, in which time we did an amazing number of singles – not actually all released at the same time – but we went in and recorded them. John's Children was literally made up of Marc Bolan singles, because he was the lyricist . . . He wrote 'Mustang Ford' and when he left, we changed the lyrics to 'Go Go Girl'. That wasn't our choice but Simon Napier-Bell's. He said we should change the lyrics to more of a 'glam' period which wasn't Glam as such during the Glitter period, but way back Napier-Bell decided that 'glam' was quite a good idea, so we changed the lyrics.

"Actually, there was a Marc Bolan number that not many people seem to know about. It was called 'Dan The Sniff'. We used to do it on stage. It's an amazing number . . . the chorus line went 'Dan (sniff), Dan (sniff), Men-thol Dan'. You sniff into the microphone, right, which was an amazing Marc Bolan thing, right – it's like 'Horrible Breath' . . . and there was 'Jasper C. Debussy' – we used to do that on stage. There was quite a lot of stuff that turned up on his first couple of albums that John's Children used to do as a heavy metal thing.

"We did a tour with The Who, and after that tour it was the end of John's Children as such because Marc left and we had all our gear confiscated. This was in Ludwigshafen in Germany. It was three German bands, John's Children, then The Who. The Who couldn't play after us because we caused such a riot. All I remember was the army moving in and us being booted offstage. I got kicked in the crotch, and as John's Children used to wear all white I had a huge great boot mark right across my trousers in the middle of my crotch! As we were driving away, all these armoured cars were driving in. What happened was we'd got towards the end of our act and I'd jumped off the stage and thrown feathers from pillows which I used to take from the hotels. And Marc put his guitar on his head and thrashed his amps with chains. And we were doing a number called

'You're A Nothing' which incorporated a Sieg Heil (we're not into Germans or anything — it was just like a repetitive chant) . . .

"That was the end of John's Children for about three months, and Marc split — it says in the press and a lot of fanzines that Marc split because of something to do with the singles — that we released them with strange things on them and he didn't like the vocals we added. But that wasn't anything to do with it. It was because John's Children split up, and he really wanted to go and form a band of his own. So he did that and John's Children reformed as a three-piece for a while, but due to disputes within the band, we split up and I eventually went to the Continent.

"When he was with John's Children he was very quiet — we were the loonies . . . when we were travelling on the road, he'd sit in the car and he'd write lyrics and be very quiet, and we'd say, 'C'mon, Marc' — you know. And when the car broke down, we'd run up the hillside and throw things and he'd still sit in the car. We used to smoke in those days and drop acid, but he'd never do anything like that. He used to take a bit of wine — but one glass did nothing. And he'd say, 'Don't worry. I'm quite high myself'. Actually, he was quite perky after gigs. For about half an hour he'd really be one of the band, but then he'd go back into the old Marc Bolan of another world.

"His guitar playing was incredibly basic. He really wasn't a good guitarist — but he moved well and made a lot of strange noises from the guitar, which was more than anyone else was doing at the time. In fact, he had some special screens made once. We turned up to one gig, and he had these metal foil screens — quite big — which folded out. He put them behind his amplifiers and he said they reflected the sound so that you could get a feedback in different places. I'm never quite sure whether it did or not. Anyway, it looked pretty good. He was just a really good singer and songwriter — not a very good guitarist — but a very distinctive voice."

Chapter 3

Marc wanted complete control and complete creative freedom so he decided to form a new band, modelled on Tomorrow, continuing from where John's Children left off. Steve Peregrine Took (who took his name from Tolkien's 'Lord Of The Rings' – essential hippy reading), was the first to join. He was 18. They met "outside a tube station". Took recalled, "I thought he ran light shows or something. I just answered an ad in International Times. We had a rehearsal, did a gig – it was dire, The Electric Garden, which is what Middle Earth was before."

There were four of them. Steve had a double drumkit and Marc still had his electric guitar and amp. They had a 28 year old bearded lead guitarist called Ben who, according to Steve, "kept turning green with stomach ulcers!" They also had a bass guitarist, also a lot older than them, who Steve recalled "smoked a pipe" which Steve believed neatly categorised him as an undesirable.

Marc named this short-lived band Tyrannosaurus Rex after the largest living creature ever to walk the earth: "It excited me to think that beasts that big walked on the earth, everyone is so unaware of things like that now. People are very much against mythology. Mythology is old truth, changed and woven, because people do that, but it's truth . . . those creatures were around, and perhaps a million years before there were dragons, they breathed fire . . . why not? I can't get together a 40 foot creature that had the earth to itself, but they have bones to prove it. If people understood that, it would make everything less hard – like their tax problems and so on, all the bummers that you go through because 90 million years ago there were those creatures around, and in 90 million years from now . . . who knows? And I like the pictures of them too."

At their first gig Tyrannosaurus Rex played both old John's Children numbers and new songs: 12-bar numbers with new words. But it was disastrous. They were incompatible. "It didn't happen – it was the wrong people", Steve explained.

"I don't know how Marc got involved with them. It was a mistake from the start . . . We couldn't afford anyone else 'cause we weren't making much money." They recruited a violinist who didn't gel either. Marc: "As a group, we didn't bother much with rehearsing. Our theory was that you just went on and told your audience what songs were coming up and did them." Track repossessed Marc's guitar and amp because he'd left John's Children so the band broke up, but Marc and Steve decided to carry on.

Steve remembered, "So then I sold me drumkit so we could pay the rent . . ." He replaced it with a small pair of bongos and Marc bought a battered £6 guitar. "As the fates would have it, a pair of bongos sufficed", Steve remarked.

Marc and Steve, now an acoustic duo, recorded demos of their new 'eastern-mystical' sound, while still tied to Track. These later appeared on the compilation 'Beginning Of Doves' along with other demos and out-takes from the period.

Simon Napier-Bell described what happened during this transitional period:

"He sort of formed T. Rex before he left John's Children. After being with them for nine months, he did that disastrous gig at the Rock Garden. It was terrible because he really was naïve. He actually got three musicians together and went to the Rock Garden, He'd never met them until that night. It was really odd because that was his answer to John's Children.

"'Beginning Of Doves' was done after that disastrous gig. He brought a rug and joss-stick and said he was going to be what he was. I said 'OK we'll go and record you' which we did. I said we really ought to do an album of this stuff because it would be cheap and could be beautifully recorded. And he said, 'I don't want it beautifully recorded, I just want to sit on the floor with one microphone.' I persuaded him to use two so it would at least be stereo. There were a lot of good bits in 'Beginning Of Doves' but it was very 'beginning stage'.

"The 'Beginning Of Doves' had solo ascoustic numbers which were the original demos I did that first session. Then there were the Tyrannosaurus Rex tracks at this much later stage. All the tracks except the solo demos were done after he left John's Children. 'Sally Was An Angel' (second half) was John's Children — I don't know why it wasn't released. We actually did an album with John's Children but Track didn't release it as they were waiting for the really monster hit single to sell it. This was a studio album with Marc not the 'Orgasm' album done before he joined. It was very good. It was very similar to what his later hits started to sound like. 'Electric Warrior' had a great similarity to that lost John's Children album. Unfortunately, when Track folded, some workmen came in and threw all the tapes on a fire and they were destroyed. There may be some acetates around though.

"All the Tyrannosaurus Rex tracks are overdubbed by Marc and Steve. There wasn't anyone else on that album. The girl's voice that you can hear very faintly at the beginning of one track was his girlfriend at that time. When his record was originally going to come out in '71 we started the whole thing off with Marc saying, 'Look, fuck off or get out' and we put that on the front and went into 'Jasper C. Debussy' and it had a great impact. It was said to his girlfriend and that's why it was to be called 'Hard On Love' originally. He really said it with viciousness, but when he was nice he was nice. He put an injunction on it and the funny thing was he said that the bit of talking at the beginning of the record was recorded when he was no longer under contract to me. He said it was recorded at a concert at Wembley. He'd mistaken it for that because I'd put a lot of echo on it to make it sound really big. He said it had been at a gig when twenty thousand teenage girls had come to see him. The judge was horrified and he lost his sympathy. We said 'He's mistaken your lordship. It was said to his girlfriend!' By then the judge was so anti-Marc that the injunction was taken off and we released it without the beginning and called it 'The Beginning Of Doves'.

"The reason he went into John's Children was because no one would accept his voice. It was Mungo Jerry that got the public to accept that voice, not him. If you listen to T. Rex just around the time Mungo Jerry had 'Summertime' as a hit, he'd just made his voice much less warbly and thinner. Mungo Jerry did this brilliant commercial song with Marc's voice and it must have killed him. All those years he had it and they took it and made it their gimmick. It was Mungo Jerry who sold Marc Bolan. They made the voice acceptable. He said 'If I had made a commercial record I'd have been as big as that.' It must really have upset him quite a lot but it was the kick he needed. He had gone away after the Decca singles and invented that voice. It was a total put-on. After the Decca thing he came to me and said 'I've invented this voice'. He literally had.

"There was a fantastic amount of stuff with John's Children. The singles weren't all recorded within a week. We were in and out of the studio all the time but the tapes got wiped after 10 years. He joined in the summer of '67 and stayed nearly till the next summer. I let him out of the contract in early 1968 after Tyrannosaurus Rex had started as I couldn't help him.

"He just wanted to sit around on a carpet and do what he was doing. He was even rejecting the idea of recording. If he was projecting himself as the unworldly hippy living off air and joss-sticks it wasn't going to do him any good having a manager. He needed to be unmanaged if he was going to have any validity."

As 1967 came to a close Marc and Steve left Track to find a new label and producer. They recorded a few demos with Joe Boyd producing and with Danny Thompson on cello. Marc thought they couldn't use the 'cello once and then not again. He knew the time would come when he could use his ideas without fear of them falling through, so he patiently built up their following by playing at universities, colleges and festivals for virtually no money just to get the exposure.

The man who helped them most during this period was disc jockey John Peel. He demanded that if *he* was booked, Tyrannosaurus Rex should be booked too. Peel had played 'Hippy Gumbo' a lot, and when he left Radio London he and Bolan quickly became firm friends. Tyrannosaurus Rex first appeared on the second 'Top Gear' show.

Marc: "I met John when he came off Radio London, and he was like us – he couldn't get any gigs. I'd just started work with Steve, who was the only survivor of four. John got a gig at Middle Earth when it opened, and we went along and played – just acoustic guitar and bongos – unamplified. Then gigs started to happen ...£10 sometimes, really heavy bread!"

John Peel remembers, "One day in

1967, Marc came round to my flat and sat on the floor and sang some of his songs. I must say they registered immediately... I knew deep down inside that he was something special. He was sort of happy, unique and rather simple in his writing style.

"I remember trying desperately to get him on to a TV programme called 'How It Is'. I kept saying 'Bolan's soon going to be producing number one hits' but they just fell about, scoffing, saying 'With that funny squeaky little voice? It'd be like having Larry the Lamb!'"

However, despite sessions on Peel's new BBC radio shows and regular gigs at Middle Earth they still didn't have a recording contract.

That is until they were happened upon by a young producer who was looking for a new group to produce for his record company as a 'token underground group'. That producer was Brooklyn-born Tony Visconti and when he walked into the Middle Earth club in 1968 he immediately saw the potential in Tyrannosaurus Rex.

Tony Visconti: "I was always interested in the freaky things, the unique music rather than the obvious. That attracted me to T. Rex. I'd never heard anything like them. I was hypnotised looking at them and so were 200 other people.

"Before we got together and started recording, Marc was very inquisitive about me and wanted to know what sort of person I was. We played guitar together and found we liked more or less the same type of music: Phil Spector, The Beach Boys and The Beatles."

After their Middle Earth set he approached Marc only to be told he was the fifth one that week.

A week later Marc arranged a contract with Regal Zonophone because they were the only company prepared to let Rex produce an album straight away. With a very small budget and only a few days to record, Tony Visconti managed to produce an album. It was a simple production as they wanted to sound live. 'My People Were Fair' was released in July 1968. A lot of the songs were quite old, mostly meant for John's Children, and others had recently been aired on Peel and Bob Harris shows.

Marc thought the first album was very bad even though Tony knew what he wanted to get across: "It was the first LP he'd ever produced and it was done at Advision on an 8-track, the first in the country, and they didn't know how to use it. The stereo was awful. When we were doing it, it sounded good, but when it was on record, it sounded very thin and nasty. But we did it in two or three sessions. I like the feeling of the first LP, but as a production, I can't listen to it."

Tony Visconti: "You can have tremendous music but if the mix is bad, people hear a poor quality record. I found that with a person like Marc Bolan, no one understood his music apart from Marc and myself. The engineers were so slow that I had to take over to make the music as good as I could."

Marc and Steve worked in a fairly well-regulated way. Steve: "Well, he just wrote a song and I did what I wanted round it. Gave it the treatment you know? We just did it in our front rooms. I played organ a

bit. I guess he wrote a lot that we never actually used, but then you do. It was very workable. We got a lot of communication going. You can when there are only two of you."

Shortly after the release of 'My People Were Fair', Marc commented on the band's unique sound: "I didn't realise it was unique. I've always sung like that really. I suppose we are trying to imitate the instruments. It's just a development of my mind. I never used to like singing but now it is a great fulfilment, like flying. I think it mirrors what I feel inside. My guardian angel does all the writing; I'm sure it's not me."

Before the album was released, Marc and Steve recorded a single, 'Debora', which they completed in one take. It was later re-recorded for the second album but the single version got to number 34 in the charts and Marc once again felt he was getting somewhere. "I was never really influenced by the chart. When 'Debora' had got in, it didn't really strike me as anything special because in those days the chart was wide open."

The album charted too but the critics didn't like it. Ray Connolly wrote in the Evening Standard, "Maddeningly monotonous; pop at its most pretentious", and in the Sunday Times Derek Jewell savaged their Queen Elizabeth concert. But Marc remained undeterred, "I really dug that Derek Jewell thing, if only because he had read the programme and quoted lyrics, and ended by calling me a poet and making comparisons about the capacity of other poets like Ezra Pound who have filled similar halls. He took the trouble to examine the event thoroughly and I respect him for that. I sent him a letter saying 'thank you' actually."

Marc was signed to Blackhill Enterprises and it was there that he met his wife-to-be, June Child. They decided to live together and it wasn't until 1970 that they got married. They lived in a small cold-water flat in Notting Hill Gate and one night as they lay in bed the Tyrannosaurus Rex picture on the wall began to move and June swore she heard the monster breathing.

Marc: "I was afraid. I knew I was afraid. I knew I was doing it. I knew my imagination had brought it to life. I also knew afterwards that had I not stopped looking at it, it would've destroyed me. The Tyrannosaurus Rex would've eaten me and there would've been blood on the bed. Since then I've been so strong I believe nothing could hurt me."

The gigs became more prestigious and better paid but the interviews were still rich in love and mystical theories: "The elphin creature to me, and according to all the reading I've done and the people I've met and all the things I know to be true, was a spiritual creature seven feet tall who had transcended the body, but had remained on Earth. He was a different make-up. We're all from different planets, right? Perhaps he was a Venusian or something, whatever, from a far-off galaxy.

"Elfin creatures are not two-inch fey creatures – they're very powerful scientific sorcerers. They're not around much any more because they can't survive in this atmosphere. Who can survive in this atmosphere? Only beasts. Which is what we are. So to me, Tyrannosaurus Rex was never a lame, camp, faggy sort of number, it was a very powerful prehistoric force."

John Peel was recruited to read two children's stories, written by Bolan. One was used on 'My People Were Fair' and the other was reserved until the third album.

The first year ended with the release of the second album: 'Prophets, Seers and Sages' which was also recorded in a short time. The single from it, 'One Inch Rock', disappeared without trace. The album, however, sold well enough for Tyrannosaurus Rex to buy stereo PA equipment.

Marc stopped using his six quid guitar with Sellotape round the neck, and bought a new Suzuki. They also bought toy organs and children's instruments, including a pixyphone!: "If I get a particular feeling, then it has to come out. I can just sit down and get a song written down straight away. It takes me as long to do as it takes to physically write it down. As soon as I start to think about it, then I might as well forget it. It has to come out unconsciously. Once I've got it down, I usually play it to myself about 20 times on the trot, getting the music worked out, and then tape it on my little recorder. Maybe we use it – maybe not."

'Unicorn' contained the haunting 'Romany Soup' – "It's something we bought in Cornwall," Marc explained, "It's made by Knorr or someone and it really tasted a groove." Marc explained about the rest of the album: "When we did it, it was very obvious to me that it was going to be the last I did with Steve – in fact, we both knew it at the time.

"We were living in Cornwall and Wales, and I was very close to the earth

... It was a period of clarity and purity – and 'Unicorn' was very much into my soul – it was all me. It was the first time I got into production as well ... like 'Romany Soup' has 22 tracks on it and took five hours to mix. On the 'Unicorn' track, the drums gave me a real buzz because I wanted to get a Phil Spector sound. I don't know how well it came off.

"I like to get a song as nearly right as I can before I play it to Steve. I like to present him with a finished thing, so that he can add exactly what he wants with his drums. We're both so in tune with each other that most things just seem to fit naturally and spontaneously.

"There are a lot of bad scenes now we're doing reasonably well. Money doesn't mean much to me, but all these people out of my past are trying to get their hands on some. You've just got to blank off to them and all the other hang-ups. Few things are really that important."

In January 1969, while still signed to Regal Zonophone, they released their third single 'Pewter Suitor'. It was another flop. The hippies weren't good record buyers and even the new album 'Unicorn' which leaned towards more simplistic ideals and had a Spectorish production didn't make any waves – although it is now regarded as the best Tyrannosaurus Rex album and a masterpiece of that period.

In May 1969 after the release of 'Unicorn', Marc took to experimenting with the electric guitar and recorded 'King Of The Rumbling Spires'. He was extremely disappointed that it too flopped.

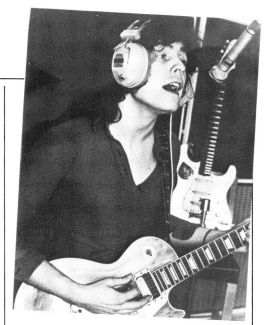

Prior to starting the ill-fated American tour on June 15th, Marc said, "We've altered very much from how we used to be. We use a full drum kit now and we have done a completely electric single. It sounds like John's Children. On the new album we use bass and a proper drum kit we bought in Hamley's. And I've bought a Stratocaster.

"It doesn't actually sound that much different, just more funky. We always played pop music anyway, and to me it's completely fair to use electricity. But we won't be loud. We're using two 15-watt amps."

Tony Visconti: "It was Marc who wanted the change. One day he turned up with an electric guitar and I knew how to handle it. I knew how to record electric guitar. If he needed bass I'd play bass for him. If he needed strings I'd write the parts for him. I covered all the directions he wanted to go in."

He compared the new 'Spires' single to The Who and then explained how they were recording at the time. "For us, eight hours is a long session. We've always had complete freedom to do what we like. I have a complete say in everything and Tony Visconti, our producer, is such a lovely cat."

After the tour Steve decided to split saying that he wanted to play guitar and do his own songs. Marc recalled: "We just grew apart. We never were that together. Steve was a really good percussionist, but when it got to expanding, we just couldn't make it work together. The one electric gig we did at the Lyceum was disastrous ...

"As a kid I always wanted to record, and it took me so long to get into records I don't want to stop now. It's silly when you see groups in studios sitting around all day, just dirtying up the place. There's no need to spend 20 hours getting a bass sound. Record it flat and 'live', then spend the time on reducing."

Marc and Steve split in the last months of 1969. Marc wanted a replacement who was a rocker at heart. He'd had enough of the jangly flower-power trips. He settled for Mickey Finn who was introduced by a mutual friend and who he met in the Seed restaurant on Westbourne Grove.

Mickey a painter by trade, had made two singles: 'I Still Want You' in 1964 as Mickey Finn & The Blue Men, and Tom Hark. Prior to joining Marc, he had been conga player with Hapshash & The Coloured Coat. Mickey described his rôle with Marc as originally being "Bongos, congas, percussion, stomp, atmosphere, dance".

They went to a cottage in Wales to rehearse the songs in order to overdub Mickey's contributions over Steve's since they couldn't have Steve on those tracks now for 'legal reasons'. But on returning to London they found that gigs were few. "Part of it was my fault," Marc explained, "But everybody was under the impression that the band had vanished, split finally. And I kept telling them that I was actually back together again . . .

"It was a long time before we really got things going. We'd this reputation before, when it was Steve and I, but when we finally did get down to some work, I doubt if anybody really noticed I had a new bloke up there with me." Not surprising really as Mickey looked so much like Steve at the beginning (take a look at the 'A Beard of Stars' cover) that Marc probably *was* the only one who knew!

Mickey picked up the bass too, and he and Marc went back into the studio to polish off 'A Beard Of Stars'. It was basically a solo album. Marc played most of the instruments as it was quicker to re-do Steve's parts himself than teach them to Mickey. But when the album was released in March 1970 it flopped. Critics said he'd "sold out", "gone electric" as if it were a crime. Marc was determined to be a star and knew that if he and Mickey remained acoustic they would fade with the hippy movement. The single 'By The Light Of The Magical Moon' released in January flopped too but Marc was happy with the way that he and Mickey were working and was looking too far ahead to be discouraged by the album and single's bad reception. Marc: "Mickey and I could pick up guitars and play for fifteen hours straight without getting bored. I could never do that with Steve.

"'A Beard Of Stars' features the first instrumentals from T. Rex as well as the new lyric songs. This LP is a lot more electric than we've done, Mickey plays bass and tablas while I play acoustic and electric guitar. Some will say we went electric because that is the usual process with those who start on acoustic and later discover what fun it is to play all they've learnt on an electric guitar. I started on amplified guitar and then went to acoustic. It never works if you try to play one type the way you play the other.

"A lot of people influenced me as I tried to improve on the electric. Eric Clapton was one. I went to see Roy Harper and he was very good, but he struck me as one who didn't quite have the feel for the electric guitar. He tried too much acoustic work on it. I thought he was great though, and I'm not even into folk music – I never was. The things that inspired me were pop music and poetry.

"I think a good pop tune is one with lyrics that mean something, instead of typical phrases. When I write, it comes from pictures inside my head – I never have to sit and think about it.

"Pop music is an art form, and, therefore, should be good music. It is important to me to have hits, I suppose, but it must be done properly. There are a lot of people in this so-called category – the underground – who consistently make the charts at about number 25, yet drop out after that. It's very hard due to the number of air-plays we get. The difference between 2,000 and 20,000 records sold a day is a lot, but we must not be that brought-down by the number of records that fail completely. Each attempt is important and if we keep trying, the charts will develop into a good cross-section of the music that is popular in the country.

"Funnily enough, I never doubted that we would work out well. It wasn't so much my ego as the gigs we were doing: you can tell when something's going to go. You know and you *feel* it, and it's got little to do with whether you're good or not . . . it's what's *happening*.

"Mickey's much more of a rock 'n' roll drummer than Steve. A lot of the numbers on the new record didn't start as riffy as they ended up; they grew into heavier things. Suddenly there was a rhythm section behind me.

"Me and Eric Clapton have played together a couple of times, which was probably what initially got me into seriously playing lead again.

"I just dragged Mickey away to Wales, where we spent a month letting things get together.

"After about a week back, we went to record. Nobody could get it straight, because I said, 'It's all together' and they said, 'What? You just broke up!' and I'd say, 'No, we've got a new group, Here we are'.

"I've got a little studio set up in the flat and Mickey comes over on his 650cc. Triumph and we just blow for a couple of hours. It's all very relaxed . . . we play together very naturally. I think we'll have a bass player at some point, but not just yet. We're playing sets of about two hours, and that's leaving out half the numbers we'd like to do, so I couldn't fit anyone else in yet. But as my ambitions guitarwise expand and Mickey gets to drum more – he's using a small kit now, not just bongos – there'll come a point where if I want to do a long guitar solo . . . or just allow something to happen like that, then we'll need a bass player for that number. I know some people who'd like to do it. We'll see if it works out.

"I always seem to have ideas long before I can carry them out. I mean T. Rex has sounded like 'A Beard Of Stars' to me for two years. I was always going to do it, you know what I mean? Even when we did 'Debora', it was always 'next week I'll plug my Stratocaster in'. But I couldn't play well enough then to make the noises that I wanted to hear.

"I tried to work out why it was that Tyrannosaurus Rex became successful. I still don't know, but there seems to be a magic behind it that's not me at all . . . there are elements that hold us together and I don't have anything to do with them at all."

The success he had at that time was frequent bookings and the continual (but minimal) sales of the albums. But Marc hadn't really tasted success at all – that was yet to come.

In February 1970 after the release of 'By The Light Of The Magical Moon' (the first single with Mickey Finn), Marc and June decided to hop down to Kensington Registry Office and get married. They'd been living together since June 1967 but just decided to 'get hitched' to 'funk up the day'. Mickey, Jeff Dexter, and friends were present at the ceremony and only one photo (snapped by a young Indian boy who happened to be passing) exists.

Chapter 4

One August evening, Marc was relaxing at home when June told him to go and write something as he was unoccupied and getting on her nerves. So he shut himself away in his little music room dampened with egg boxes, and got down to writing. The next morning June brought in some coffee and Marc played her the tape he'd made. The song was called 'Ride A White Swan'. A session was already booked for that afternoon so Marc decided to try it out. For the first time on a Bolan song strings were added. They were arranged by Tony Visconti who still retained the Denny Cordell style from the old Move days, but it gelled really well. It was decided that this new direction would be as good a time as any to abbreviate the name officially and so T. Rex was born.

"For three years I didn't do anything visually. I played sitting down all the time, never moved, didn't move a muffle! [sic] But we had big albums and we were what I thought was successful at the time. The credibility of the band was lessened by the fact that people associated us with flower power, and that was a long-gone era. I wanted people to look at the thing in a new light, and the only way to do that was to have a label change, and change the music, and change the name, but not lose any identity either way. I make it sound very controlled but it wasn't, it all happened in three days, and I got put on Fly records. I didn't choose to be there. Legally that happened because the company I was with signed with those people who formed Fly records.

"The music grew through three albums to what it is now, and people did all that bullshit about instant overnight electricity, which was ludicrous because it had taken two and half years. From 'Unicorn' onwards it's very obvious."

'Ride A White Swan' was backed with 'Is It Love?' and a version of Eddie Cochran's 'Summertime Blues', the only non-original T. Rex released until 1975. Bolan's B-sides were always as good, if not better, than his A-sides and the new policy of giving three tracks instead of the usual two was a wise move both artistically and commercially.

George Tremlett described his impression on meeting Marc: "It was around the time 'Ride A White Swan' came out. I was asked to write an article for 'Teenage' magazine and I met him in an office in the King's Road which was the home of E.G. Management, Enthoven and Gaydon, who were then his agents.

"The thing I remember particularly was that he was wearing a blanket around him that was supposed to be a cloak but which was obviously a cut-up blanket. I liked him, I genuinely liked him because he had a gift for words.

"Mickey Finn had one of the best gifts for language of anyone I'd ever met, he had a better facility for words than Marc Bolan himself. Marc Bolan was very career conscious, determined to sell a lot of records, determined to be a star. He was very careful not to let people around him become too prominent – understandable – but in Mickey Finn's case it did him a considerable injustice. Marc was a very dominant person.

"About the first time he was developing a relationship with Gloria, I asked him, as part of the things that the paper wanted me to ask, what was it about her that attracted him. He grinned and said, 'I always liked black pussy didn't I', that was a typical comment. My wife was there and he gave her a wicked wink. He was totally natural. He respected his audience. He put out records to sell, he cared though about what he was doing.

"David Bowie certainly recognised what was there, he could see it. I don't think many of the Press could. I don't think anything just comes. You've got to have almost superhuman drive and I think he had that. He worked bloody hard for it.

"His book of poems, 'Warlock Of Love', I think is very good. It's a bit obtuse, it's very Dylan Thomas. I once put it to him about this and drew the allusions, the actual compositions and the derivation. He wasn't livid but he wasn't amused. He disagreed strongly, but there's nothing wrong in having roots, nothing wrong in having influences."

When T. Rex toured a few days after 'Swan's' release, Marc made another shrewd move. He set a maximum ticket price of 50p, a move later to be adopted by other groups such as Led Zeppelin and The Stones.

The fans that came to Rex concerts were now becoming younger. The hippies were being replaced by singles buyers and this unique duo began to appeal to the imagination of the stale music press. Bolan was a gifted and original songwriter, his voice and presentation were unique and he was highly photogenic. When they began to interview him (Mickey was rarely interviewed, preferring a low profile), they found an intelligent and witty little guy who had a new quote for every journalist and

obviously knew his rock 'n' roll.

That first week of the tour, 'Ride A White Swan' was reviewed by John Peel in Disc. "As God-like I strode the forecourt and a small voice hailed from a vehicle which lay mute and lifeless beneath the harsh lights. Drawing my noble sword, Renshaw, I was across the concrete in a trice to find that my tiny friends, T. Rex were becalmed. Chuckling, I scooped them up in the palm of a soft pile of green stamps and bore them so to London town. As we sped straight and true to that fair city, they told me of their concert tour, of the new record 'Ride A White Swan' on Fly records. Doubtless you'll own it before long – if you don't by Christmas, my flock of highly trained hedgehogs will fan out through the land and retribution will be swift and terrible – indeed it will . . ."

'Ride A White Swan' was played initially only once on Radio One but in the next few days it sold over 20,000 copies, and then every shop seemed to be playing it. It was put on the BBC playlist. John Peel's little prodigées and Fly's 'token underground group' had become the darlings of early seventies singles pop.

'Ride A White Swan' reached No. 2 in the singles chart and Marc, who just before its release had declared to June that it was 'make or break this time', and who would have become a 'wandering poet' if it had flopped, was not going to let success slip through his fingers again.

"The success of 'White Swan' is a gas," commented Marc in November 1970, "because I want people to hear my music. We could be very comfortable just being an underground act . . . quite well established, doing concert tours, selling a fair amount of each album . . . but it is not really on.

"You get to the stage where you have had four or five albums and you begin to feel you are not reaching people. I know for a fact that 'White Swan' is getting to people who have never been interested before and maybe some of them will buy the next album."

He had his own pop philosophy. "I've suddenly tuned into that mental channel which makes a record a hit and I feel at present as though I could go on writing number ones forever. Let's face it, the majority of pop hits that make it are a permutation on the 12-bar blues and I've found one that works.

"I've never felt so insecure or such pain as I do now with my music because I am so exposed – it's straight projection and giving of my real self, but that's all I really care about. The people I have always admired – like Hendrix and Clapton – have that ability to give something so soulful, a personal sense of urgency that you communicate through the music . . .

"I couldn't believe it the first time I went out on stage and saw all those little white faces. No one is going to convince me that their enthusiasm is a bad thing for Rex. If there is going to be any revolution in pop, it must come from the young people and if you ignore them you are cutting yourself off from the life-supply of the rock music force."

Apart from the freshness in his music, his breakthrough must be attributed to the gimmick which kept the interest at a peak: his make-up and glitter around the eyes which were outrageously new in 1971. Marc claimed he'd just stuck some glitter under his eyes before a 'Top Of The Pops' appearance for a laugh and forgotten about it. At the next concert, half the audience had glitter under their eyes. Bolan, with his whimsy and sense of theatre, had started 'Glam rock' single handedly. He added touches of eyeshadow and became the hottest property this side of The Beatles. Now everybody wanted an interview, not just the weekly music press.

"I don't really care what people think," he told a journalist, shocked at his use of make-up. "If the thing works, it works. Elvis Presley wore eye make-up for years. People thought he had dark sultry eyes. Mick Jagger has wonderful skin embellishment. People are really works of art and if you have a nice face you might as well play about with it. It gets boring otherwise. Two hundred years ago, men covered themselves with something scented or wore powdered wigs and faces. If someone is prudish enough not to realise that it's all been done before they're very stupid. Anyway I don't believe chicks like really butch guys – apart from wrestlers. Valentino was living proof of that. He really was the biggest star that Hollywood turned out and he

was hardly butch was he?"

He explained the dramatic change which now occurred in his music: "All we are doing is strengthening the songs . . . if they have any strength at all. I do write quite strong melodies actually but, treated acoustically, the melody isn't so recognisable. 'Ride A White Swan' is a melodic song and it can be picked up because it has the guitar. I know what people want and I need the media. Otherwise it is like writing songs and never putting them out. I am pleased to be on Radio One and 'Top Of The Pops' because they are all we have.

"Basically, I am a hard person to work with. I am eccentric. I am very temperamental. The reason John's Children didn't work was because I couldn't cope with four people. I have no time for tensions in groups."

The next album, simply titled 'T. Rex' was released in December 1970 and charted. Howard Kaylan and Mark Volman of The Mothers of Invention (and previously with The Turtles) guested on backing vocals on 'Seagull Woman'. Marc had met them on the last American tour and they formed a friendship that was to last three years. On 'T. Rex', Mickey and Marc were still playing all the instruments although some of the burden was put on to the strings, featured on their album for the first time and expertly arranged by Tony Visconti.

By now Marc had plans for a new album and a new sound that was only previewed on 'Swan'. ". . . I've got this sound in my head that is definitely unlike anything else we have put out. It really is cosmic rock. I'd like to catch on the record the essence of the audiences we are getting so that people will know what is happening. People who've come to gigs really cannot believe it. It really is like the old rock days . . . people rushing the stage. Right now we're about the only band with stereo equipment on the road. As we earn a bit more money, so we plough it back into better equipment so we can give the fans a better sound."

The ten-shilling tour was a great innovation but Marc knew he would have to have a rock band behind him to keep the younger audience – and to become a star, the thing he most wanted and was determined to attain. He recruited bass player Steve Currie, an ex-shipping office clerk who was an excellent musician having played five years with jazz-rock bands.

Steve Currie: "I'd been through a whole load of Mickey Mouse bands. I knew Tony Visconti who was a record producer and a friend of Marc's who'd played a couple of dates with them filling in on bass. He took me down to watch Marc and Mickey play a couple of gigs and I could tell something was missing; that they needed a tight rhythm section behind them for the kind of numbers they were doing.

"To be honest, I didn't really want to join them. There was such an aura around Marc, I thought he was some kind of a freak and I just couldn't imagine myself working with him at all. I thought I'd go back to driving a lorry where I was happy – I didn't want to get up in it at all."

But Steve soon changed his mind and was hired when he found he liked the new direction Marc intended to take. Then Marc started to audition drummers, originally just for the next single session.

Publicist B.P. Fallon: "It was quite amazing. We had Australians who had just landed here, kids of 12, people who didn't have any equipment, people who didn't even have any drumsticks."

Steve Currie: "These people would come in and search for Marc's face. I think a lot of them thought it was all a big put-on when they didn't see him there. The standard was really terrible because the name attracted a lot of wrong people. There were only about three guys that were any good and if anyone was okay I'd say 'hold on a minute' and then dash out to bring Marc back to listen."

Bill Legend, one of the three Steve

dragged Marc back to hear: "I'd split up this band I'd been playing in and to be honest I just needed some work. I'd never heard of T. Rex." He got the job.

Expanding the group wasn't as instant a decision as it first appeared. Marc: "I thought about it for a long, long time. In the beginning I was totally opposed to it, like I usually am to anything anyone suggests. Beep (B.P. Fallon) once said to June that we'd be really incredible if we had a bass player, but I just didn't want to know about it. Then someone else said that if we had bass and drums we'd be one of the biggest groups in the world but it was instant block, I just didn't want to know.

"Then I started thinking about it . . . I was overdubbing like mad on all the records and I wasn't really getting the feeling I wanted. There was a great gap. And then it struck me really hard and I just couldn't do another gig without a bass player. Tony Visconti played bass on two gigs, we blew out another four, and auditioned for a bass. We got Steve. He was the first we interviewed and he was dynamic. So we worked for two weeks like that and then realised that if Mickey wanted to get into congas, which he did, we'd have to get a kit drummer. I knew a guy called Bill, who was in Legend, and we did a couple of days rehearsal with him and off we went. His real name is Bill Fyfield, but we always used to call him Bill Legend. We nicked Legend's roadie too, so I bet they hate me."

They auditioned a lot of drummers over a number of days. Marc: "About four days I think, but after a while I did a typical Bolan cop-out and left Steve in there while I played billiards next door. For the first two, I was really enthusiastic and spoke for hours, but in the end we didn't choose any of them. They were all good, but not what I wanted. It was their heads I was looking at, not their playing . . . I was looking inside them, and not one fitted. Bill was perfect. All I've done really is re-create John's Children, or what I wanted John's Children to be when I was with them at the beginning, and I'm writing exactly the same stuff as I was five years ago . . . It's no different except that it's a bit better, hopefully, and has a bit more insight. But I can play it now and I couldn't before . . . I could only play 'Desdemona'."

The new single was a pure teenage bopping single: 'Hot Love'. Howard Kaylan and Mark Volman sang backing vocals and there were a lot of friends and guests who joined in with backing vocals and handclaps at the end. 'Hot Love' had lyrics that didn't really mean anything but sounded so right. It was a mixture of Dion, Buddy Holly and Elvis Presley spliced in with a reworked coda from 'Hey Jude' and some 1970's 'Cosmic Rock'. It was an instant commercial success, and became Marc's first number one single, staying at the top for six weeks.

"I never thought consciously about things like word choices in any of my old songs — I only thought about the feeling. 'Hot Love' I wrote because I wanted to write a rock record — I know it's exactly like a million other songs, but I hope it's got a little touch of me in it too. It was done as a happy record, and I wanted to make a 12-bar record a hit, which hasn't been done since 'High Heeled Sneakers' really . . . though I wasn't sure that it would be a hit. What happened was that we got very lushed one night, had about four bottles of brandy, it was about four in the morning, and we just did it — I wasn't aware that it was going to be such a big record . . . I just dug it, that's all."

Marc appeared on 'Top Of The Pops' in satin jacket and bright satin trousers and the whole audience imitated him. They were supported by new band, Genesis (!), and at such venues as the Brighton Dome they could have filled the hall three times over with the people waiting outside. There were riots the like of which had never been seen in Britain since The Beatles.

Kids were attracted by the new T. Rex sound: a fresh brand of rock 'n' roll with the distinctive mellow Bolan voice, more restrained than the old style undergound wobble. It was just what was needed in the stale atmosphere of the early seventies.

"In our case, initially, I was trying to get away from the pop syndrome and, for me, the underground at the beginning meant similar minded people with similar thoughts. I now really do think that the progressive era has borne fruit when you have groups like T. Rex, Family, Fairport, etc., getting hit records in the

same breath as people like Gerry Monroe and Shirley Bassey.

"Of course, as it got more of a business, managers realised that if you called your group progressive then you automatically had an audience. And for a time the audience was gullible enough to accept a group called, let's say, Ramasses Bullet and presume they were really good . . . I am sure one could do a Monkees with any group. Give them a pretty name, a handsome looking lead guitarist and you're off, man. You're a millionaire."

Marc had been learning to project his star image. When asked how long it took to write 'Hot Love', he tossed back his black locks and off-handedly answered, "Ten minutes . . . didn't even think about it". This arrogant but impish remark angered many of his critics and the expansion of the group and the enviable chart success of 'Hot Love' had critics making accusations of a sell-out.

But Marc never sold out. He was always true to himself. If people liked his writing it meant that they thought as he did and could identify with him and T. Rex. Letters of Bolan "selling out to the cosmos" appeared in the press. "On live gigs we haven't had one bad vibe . . . not one . . . about 10 people may have written in, but the sad thing is that I know for a fact that at least 40 or 50 good letters were sent in and didn't get printed. It's

nobody's fault – it's just the twentieth century, and I have to accept it whether I like it or not . . . I don't like it, but there you are.

"We're big business now . . . after three and a half years or so of funking along, doing all right and, in fact, no different from what we're doing now, we just happened to grow in a way that became acceptable to a wider public . . . as did rock 'n' roll. But I think that practically any of our old songs could be a top 5 hit now – now that people have got used to us.

"My interest now is getting to people's heads and hearts, and relating to their love lives, their problems, what pain they feel . . . that's all I care about. I mean, in the last two years or so, I've had a fucking awful lot of pain – we all have, because we're in the right age in a problem world. That's all I'm into, and if people don't understand that, then they're not mature enough to feel pain – in which case, I don't care about them anyway.

"I'm a much more sexually extrovert person than I ever was and naturally that's affecting what I'm writing. I haven't stopped writing the kind of things we were doing before but I'm doing it in the form of poetry, and words to read as opposed to putting them into my songs. There's still that side of me to come out through some channel.

"I've never done anything in music that I didn't honestly believe in so I don't believe I've ever let any of my fans down. I even look pretty much the same as I did. My hair's a bit longer and I look a bit more haggard – but there's really very little difference. So I just couldn't understand why all those letters came in and the original Rex fans seemed so hurt. The strange thing is, had I not done what I did when I did it, I would have probably ended up as another James Taylor playing acoustic and singing gentle little songs."

His songwriting had changed to suit his new style. "Well it's matured in relevance to the society we live in – that's what I hope. You see, I'm no longer interested in abstract thought – I'm now living my fantasy . . . I am what I used to write about on those old albums – I am that. So I don't have to write about it any more . . . I see everyone as those images. At that time I was just a very young boy who had some sort of talent – or perhaps I didn't, it all depends on where you're sitting. I now live that incarnation. I see life something like a Fellini film – my head is that way – so I don't have to write like that any more. Now I try to hit into the middle of what human beings are all about. To me, it's the only important thing . . . but I don't care if I'm a road sweeper tomorrow, but two years ago I would have . . . so that's a growth. Two years ago I was very into being a poet and I'm not any more because I am a poet. I don't have to think about it. I've become Marc Bolan, in fact, which I never was before."

Chapter 5

Marc's long-awaited and inevitable break into the big time occurred during the last few months of his term with Fly Records. After the February 1971 release of 'Hot Love', Fly put out a compilation, originally to be called 'The Golden Hits of T. Rex', but retitled simply 'The Best of T. Rex', since they knew that in October Marc would be free to negotiate a new contract and move on.

This 'second break' was to help Marc become one of the richest rock superstars of the seventies and enabled him to set up his own record label and publishing company – Wizard Productions and Warrior Music Projects, which were then distributed through EMI. However, he was still committed to make one more single and album for Fly.

On July 2 that last single, 'Get It On' was released and a month later came the album, 'Electric Warrior'. The single was another number one and became a multi-million seller. It was Marc's only big American hit.

'Electric Warrior' . . . "We recorded about six tracks in Los Angeles, four in New York and two over here . . . Tony Visconti was on holiday in America so he was able to produce it.

"I wanted Howard and Mark (Kaylan and Volman from The Mothers) to be on it, and they were in America. On some of the tracks, I hadn't rehearsed the band and I didn't want to – I just wanted to go into the New York studio, very stoned, go through a number about four times, and then do the take . . . whereas in the past I used to do about 15 takes.

"As far as I'm concerned, it's the first album I've ever made; the others were just ideas, but in this one I spoke about me, and you, and all of us.

"Howard and Mark are just incredible singers; when they came over with The Mothers, we recorded 'Seagull Woman', then when they came over for '200 Motels' we did 'Hot Love', and they are on 'Get It On' too. 'Get It On' which was lifted from 'Electric Warrior', was an instant smash hit and stayed at number one in England for four weeks."

Howard Kaylan: "Bolan is a really fine guy and his wife June is one of THE finest ladies ever. We met Marc when he first came over here with Tyrannosaurus Rex. We went to a place in Detroit as The Turtles, and Marc and Steve Took were downbill to us. They were feeling low because they couldn't meet anybody they could relate to. We invited them back to our hotel and showed them what life on the road could be like. We talked for hours and had a good time. We left by saying that if we ever came to London we'd look them up." And they did too. They knocked at Marc's door in 1969.

"He was in and what followed was just magic between us", continued Howard. "Shortly after, Marc decided to go electric and Took flipped out, 'Pink Fairied' his way into oblivion and vanished. Well, we just had this thing with Marc, I sang on that album 'T. Rex' and then we cut 'Hot Love' with him. The next time around, all of the 'Electric Warrior' album – 'Bang A Gong' and stuff, and then 'Slider'.

"Now I think he did most of 'Slider' in France, or Denmark or somewhere. But we got a call from him in LA. 'Hey man what are you doing here?' we said. 'What do you think I'm doing here, I've got my tapes man and I want you', said Marc. So we went right down to his studio and did eight tracks. He didn't use two and we told him they were the best tracks, but . . ."

Mark Volman: "He kept telling us he was going to be super big."

Howard: "Oh yeah, now Marc isn't one of the most humble guys we've ever met – but neither are we so that gives us a really good rapport."

Mark Volman: "Yeah, and he don't give us any bull because Marc baby knows that he didn't have a hit record until we sang on his records."

Howard: "He knows that WE made him everything that he is. So everything has worked out real well" (much laughter). "A very shrewd little elf. Very shrewd," concludes Howard.

Marc's contract with EMI allowed him to hold his tapes; so EMI could issue only the material offered to them by Marc. This is why all the tracks left over from the 1972-77 albums have never been issued.

But meanwhile back in 1971 . . . Marc described writing 'Get It On': "The actual backing track of guitar, drums, and bass, Howard, Mark and I took about 10 minutes, then we double tracked which took about another five. But what we did was bring the track back from America, overdubbed Ian MacDonald on saxes, and the strings were an afterthought really. We'd put strings on the B-side, had some time over, and decided to put strings on 'Get It On' too. The only thing that took time was the lead guitar track – I did four which I wasn't happy with, then I did it again at Advision and managed to get what I wanted. The trouble was that I was playing too much, overplaying all the time, and it took some time to work that part out. Rick Wakeman did a piano part on it too . . . just came in, heard it, and played . . . took about five minutes and that was it . . ."

"I wanted to record 'Little Queenie' but it wouldn't have worked again, so I wrote my own song to it. I put that on the end so someone like you would know and wouldn't say 'What a cunt, Bolan, ripping off 'Little Queenie' because in the end, it's only the feel of the song.

"If I have a special idea on how I want to use a song I'm quite dictatorial, but if I don't I give the song to Tony and see what comes out of it. 'Cosmic Dancer' was a track I did that way and I thought the arrangements were amazing."

T. Rex included acoustic numbers on all their albums until 1975: "If people hadn't liked us going into electric rock, then I couldn't have gone on. Same as when a guy in America heckled me from out front when I had the new group line-up. Yet I went on including acoustic material to help the audiences accept the changes in what we were doing. Anyway, I like to play acoustically . . . despite being a real old rock'n'roller at heart.

Marc tried to capture the freshness, excitement and feel of the early Sun records and on 'Electric Warrior' he succeeded; some tracks were just rough backing tracks that he overdubbed because the feel of them was so good. But he wasn't completely finished with the Tyrannosaurus Rex ideas. He still had a project left to do called 'The Children of Rarn' which he'd started back in 1969. (Some tracks from 'A Beard Of Stars' and 'T. Rex' were originally written for it and 'Swan' was also to be included.) In October 1971 he recorded a demo with just a Spanish guitar at Tony Visconti's flat. Though plans were made for a double album, Marc wanted to give his audience a rock album each year and it wasn't until 1978 that it was finally released with

Visconti's string arrangements overdubbed.

In January 1971 Marc spoke of his plans for it . . . "I'm working on a musical science fiction story that I've written. The story is done, I'm just working on the medium for presenting it. I'd like to film it and do it live. The story is called 'The Children of Rarn' and concerns a complete civilisation which existed on earth before the prehistoric monsters arrived. It's a straight story — nothing ambiguous about the lines. It's got a lot of what I really believe in it — I'm not pompous enough to say it teaches, but it contains my beliefs. This won't be any Hollywood thing; I'd like to do it as a TV film — but no times have been fixed to work on it yet. I hope I'm not bored with it before it's done."

Marc was very pleased when 'Electric Warrior' was received so well by critics and public alike. It became the number one album of the year and was the first of Marc's big selling albums — establishing T. Rex as the major force on the British music scene for the next two years.

"We've got a really raunchy guitar sound and we cut tracks in a way that they can't now be altered. There is no way I can blow the energy on them, by looking at them later and being in a different mood . . . it is instant 'hum-the-songs', but the words of the songs are such that in no way can it be a sell-out. The words are very personal to the way I live. Like Neil Young . . . everything he writes is so much a pop song, but the words mean so much. 'Electric Warrior' might appear simple on the surface but it has a lot of little 'sneakies' in there if you want to dig deeper.

"It's probably the loosest album I've ever recorded because it was done between gigs in America and I was essentially concerned with putting down rough tracks to establish a sound, but they felt so good that we kept them for the finished track. It's a highly communicable album and that is the name of the game as far as I'm concerned . . . but there are some really worthwhile things on that album you can get into if you put your headphones on — backward guitar, baroque strings . . .

"I mean I am my fantasy. I am the 'Cosmic Dancer' who dances his way out of the womb and into the tomb on 'Electric Warrior'. I'm not frightened to get up there and groove in front of six million people on TV because it doesn't look cool. That's the way I would do it at home. I'm serious about the music but I'm not serious about the fantasy . . . I'm a rock'n'roll poet man who is just bopping around on the side . . . I've always been a wriggler. I just dig dancing. It was just a bit difficult to wriggle when I was with Peregrine sitting cross-legged on the stage . . .

Y'know, it's really ironic that if I had made an album like 'Unicorn' today, the critics would really have got into the words and the motivations whereas when it was issued it got put down for being pretentious jive. In today's critical climate it would be regarded as a masterpiece!"

In England Marc and T. Rex were taken as 'the new Beatles' "Once at Boston in Lincolnshire, we had everything that could possibly be snatched from our bodies taken as we made our way back to the dressing rooms. Often our cars get stripped by the girls who want to take away souvenirs. Headlights, windscreen wipers, hubcaps and doorhandles are all taken.

"I like being loved. Isn't it nice for people to care for you? Isn't it nice that someone can like you enough to put your picture on the bedroom wall? After seven years of trying to do something, having actually done it is a very strange feeling.

"The frightening thing is the sheer strength of it all but I know they don't want to hurt me. If things look really as if they are getting out of hand I feel I could stop playing, hold my hand up and ask them to steady down, and I'm sure they would.

"Apart from gigs, I've become a recluse. Weeks go by and and I don't leave the house. My life is like a goldfish bowl. Private life? I don't have one. Because it's impossible to get out and mix like most people. I'm beginning to feel a lack of contact."

In November 1971, having completed his contractual obligations with Fly, Marc began negotiations with EMI. But while the new T. Rex label was being discussed Fly records released a single of two tracks off 'Warrior' against Marc's wishes: 'Jeepster' coupled with 'Life's A Gas'. He appeared on Top Of The Pops and reluctantly promoted it. It reached number two but wasn't really an official T. Rex release.

"The story behind 'Jeepster' – that was done for the 'Electric Warrior' album right, and we did that in New York in the studio that Paul Simon did 'The Boxer'. And all those bits on it, that like dun dun dun bop bop is me banging on the floor. It had a real wooden floor like a cathedral. So it's got this bit of tap dancing on it."

While in this stalemate position, Marc was asked to contribute a track for a charity album of 'Glastonbury Fayre' called 'When The Sound Of The Music Changes'. He donated an acoustic demo of 'Sunken Rags' recorded at his home on a Revox which wasn't released in electric form until 1973, on the 'Tanx' album.

Chapter 6

On January 1, 1972 Marc signed a three year contract with EMI to release his records under the T. Rex Wax Company banner. In that same month, T. Rex were voted the world's number one group in the New Musical Express and the first release on the Wax Company Banner was put out.

'Telegram Sam' coupled with 'Cadillac' and 'Baby Strange' was the official follow-up to 'Get It On' and this pure slice of America, gleaned from their tour experience there, became T. Rex's second number one.

In February they began another extensive tour of the States, this time topping the bill and finishing with a memorable night at Carnegie Hall in New York City.

Fly released another compilation, 'Bolan Boogie' which featured tracks from both Tyrannosarus Rex and early T. Rex. It immediately became another number one album.

Marc: "I have a feeling all the time of being pinned against the wall by hundreds of invisible people. All the time. Consequently, I totally retreat. I don't go out any more, ever.

"The thing about success, certainly in the rock'n'roll business, is that it gives an incredible amount but what it takes away is irreplaceable. It's like if you take acid, it burns out brain cells, and they don't regrow. It's killing more people musically and mentally than I've ever seen it do before . . .

"Rock'n'roll is all-productive for the consumer, all-destructive for the producer. You get fabulous things materially – but then what? Sometimes I get a funny feeling inside me that I shan't be here very long, and I'm not talking in terms of things like success. It frightens me sometimes.

"I sometimes feel I know too much about life and this business than it's healthy to know. I'm becoming aware of a kind of madness inside me. But I don't want to go into all that gee-life-is-hard-at-the-top bit because I'm enjoying it. It's what I've always wanted since I was 14 and now I've got it, it's too late to back off."

Meanwhile Marc and the band were recording their new album at Elton John's favourite studio at the time, the 'Honky Château' in France: "Originally we worked in Denmark. We did 'Telegram Sam' and all that stuff over there. I first got interested in recording in Paris when I heard Paul Simon had done some things there. Also Reg was pleased with the studio. I think he did something off 'Madman Across The Water' there, then of course there was the 'Honky Château' album.

"So I decided to go over myself and check things out. First of all, we did 'Metal Guru' there. Then we finished off 'The Slider'."

'The Slider' was the new T. Rex album and it was recorded in a very short time prior to rehearsals for two concerts at the Empire Pool, Wembley. "The good thing about working at that studio is that if you are limited to just three days over there and you know you want to get a certain number of tracks down, you do it. I kept it pretty strict. We'd get in about ten and have breakfast. Then until about two, we'd be goofing about and literally going through numbers. After lunch we'd really do it. Maybe we'd go through until two the next morning."

The press fell over themselves in the rush to interview the first superstar since The Beatles and Marc so obviously enjoyed his success that some critics found it very easy to dislike him and back up their bias by pulling his off-the-wall lyrics apart. They were less 'story-like'. "That's because I think the world is very different now. I feel that what a poet should do is write down what there is . . ."

Name-dropping was the biggest characteristic of the interviews he gave at the time and it was his desperate desire to be mentioned in the same breath as John Lennon or Bob Dylan that turned a lot of people against him. "On 'Cold Turkey' Lennon was trying to sound like me. I mean he told me. If you listen to 'Live Peace: Toronto', at the end of 'Cold Turkey' Lennon says to Yoko, 'I couldn't get *that* voice'."

During this hiatus in March, Marc was planning a science fiction film, having dropped 'The Children Of Rarn', animated cartoon film and album due to other recording and touring commitments.

"It will take three months to do it the way I would like. It's about a cosmic Messiah. Not a Jesus image at all. He's a sort of messenger from God who has to check up on planet Earth. He's visually very incredible and has to adapt to be able to walk about. Really we will be filming his reactions to all the shit we take quite naturally, like garbage on the telly and mass murders and all the rubbish he has never seen before. When they left Earth it was a Garden of Eden with potential gods, and in the story God has not returned to the planet since then. He expects a race of gods and what he finds is this mess. It's basically about the reactions and disgust that this man feels. At the end of the film he is totally destroyed by the crap he sees . . . I don't know if I'll be in it, but there'll certainly be a sequence with the band."

In fact the film was dropped in favour of a movie for Apple Films based around the Wembley gigs two weeks later. On March 18, 1972 at the Empire Pool there were two sell-out performances to 100,000 people each. The fans rushed the stage, crushing the barriers and creating the first scenes of mass hysteria since the early sixties. Ringo Starr combined with Marc to finance and make the movie as T. Rex was his favourite group at the time. To the hundreds of feet of footage of Wembley, Ringo and Marc added bits of accidental humour and some footage of jamming at the Abbey Road studios. On December 14, 1972, 'Born To Boogie' was given its première.

In the interim, Fly re-released 'Debora' and B.P. Fallon, one of the greatest publicists of the rock world, quit as Marc's publicist. He had taken the job to make Marc one of the biggest stars of all time and having achieved this he felt he should leave and help someone else's career.

"Things change around you when you

50

become successful. I've not changed as a person. I've never not spoken to someone. I didn't sack B.P. (Fallon). He left. He wanted to leave very badly. He felt he had done what he wanted to do. We'd been through the beginning of the thing to the growth, and he was just like coming in and talking to the Sheffield Standard or something.

"But I was very sad. It was not an artist-press agent relationship which is why I didn't replace him." In fact Marc continued to see Beep (as he was almost affectionately called) and only weeks before Marc's death, Beep was accompanying Bolan on some home demos (clicking his fingers and clapping on '21st Century Stance').

The second T. Rex single on their own label was released on May 5 1972. 'Metal Guru' coupled with 'Lady' and 'Thunderwing' became T. Rex's fourth number one and the album 'The Slider' followed it to the top when released on July 23. It sold 100,000 copies in the first four days. Sales could have been lessened by Track's attempt to release 'Hard On Love', a compilation of early tracks that was eventually released in 1972 as 'The Beginning Of Doves' but Marc issued a high court writ and the album was shelved.

The court case sapped Marc's creative spirit and 'The Slider' nearly didn't come out. "That court case business really destroyed me. I had two weeks when I was such a mess 'cause I'd never felt like that before. I was changing managers at the time and I was very emotional. I'd cut all the tracks for 'Slider' and I just said, 'Screw it!' I did a Brian Wilson. I said, 'Fuck the album!' Don't wanna put it out. I just don't wanna record ever again!. And I went away for about a week, came back and played the tapes and thought they were great. It doesn't need promoting. I feel it's like my 'Imagine' album. It's the only album in which I've said what I think I am."

During the US tour of September and October a new single 'Children Of The Revolution' coupled with an electric version of 'Sunken Rags' and the new 'Jitterbug Love' was released. They were

recorded in Paris and proved again that Marc's B-sides were as good if not better than his A-sides.

Unfortunately, after having reached his zenith at Wembley, Marc's halo began to slip. 'Children Of The Revolution' only reached number two and broke his string of number ones. It wasn't as good as the version in 'Born to Boogie'. It was too heavy and plodding. It scored only by the spell Marc still wove; and new faces were now appearing on the scene, stealing the limelight – The Osmonds, Cassidy and most notably Bowie – who played acoustic guitar on 'Rabbit Fighter' and sang on other tracks on 'The Slider'. Bowie was influenced a great deal by Bolan and their friendship grew with the years. On Bowie's 1972 album 'Ziggy Stardust' there is a song about Marc – 'Lady Stardust' and when Bowie performed the song a screen projected an image of Marc's face in white and 'Electric Warrior' was played before he took the stage.

Rosalind Russell of Record Mirror:

"They were very friendly in the early days and used to hang out a lot together. After Bowie made it I think Marc regretted the fact that he wasn't very close to him because Bowie just grew away from everybody in this country. When Bolan said he was going to get Bowie over here to do his TV show everybody laughed. I think Marc was surprised himself when he came and did it. I was surprised, I didn't think he'd do it. Bowie said to me in the very first interview I did with him, after he had come out of that obscurity that followed 'Space Oddity' that Bolan had opened a lot of doors for him and made that comeback possible. I think Bowie respected Bolan and was grateful to him for that.

During November T. Rex made a memorable tour of the Far East and Australia, starting in Tokyo where they began recording. The next single 'Solid Gold Easy Action' was released on December 1st and only reached number four. However, the film 'Born to Boogie' was a great success.

"What it is is the best of the concerts and a lot of Ringo and me goofing about, a couple of studio things and just bits and pieces all stuck together in a way that's stimulating to the body and soul, I hope . . . it's a rock'n'roll film. It's made for the kids to rock'n'roll in the aisles. If you go and see all those old rock'n'roll films you'll see that they are all padded to death. There's no padding in this film. There is no story either."

Marc and Ringo became firm friends and Marc played on 'Have You Seen My Baby' and 'Back Off Boogaloo'.

In December 1972 two T. Rexmas specials were held, one at the Sundown, Edmonton and the other at the Sundown, Brixton.

"I've already started a second film, I'm doing a silent movie with Ringo. At the moment we're just goofing about, but we will do another film definitely."

Chapter 7

As 1973 began Marc appeared on 'The Cilla Black Show' miming to 'Mad Donna' from the forthcoming 'Tanx' album and in an acoustic duet with Cilla.

"No one expected us to do the show. I knew Cilla and her husband from quite a way back. I took some persuading to do it, but I think she's a good singer and I think it might break some sort of barrier. It was a problem but we came back and watched it on the video machine and I've played it through a lot of times and I enjoyed it. The only thing I didn't like was that I did so much wiggling about that I was out of breath when I did the second song. It was out of place but that's why we did it."

On March 2, 1973 a new T. Rex single was released: 'Twentieth Century Boy' backed with 'Free Angel' featuring Howie Casey on saxophone and backing vocals by a group of girl singers.

Marc: "Basically the content is erection rock, and like a track on the 'Tanx' album, 'Shock Rock' it's purely an energy record, and if you listen to the words it quotes from a lot of people including Mohammed Ali. I think that every young man in the 20th Century is a superstud and the record is meant for him.

"It's a funky sound compared to records that I think are really good. No more, no less. I've played it a lot of times and it still gets me off.

"Marc Bolan is changing, it's just that people aren't really listening. The kids are, they know and they are still buying the records. We're three years on now, man, twenty-four million records. I wanna do something special."

'Tanx' was released on March 16 after seven months in the making and a cost of £12,000 in studio time alone. It was recorded in France and Denmark and contained a re-wording of the unreleased John's Children song 'Mad Donna'.

The new album was an answer to the critics who were predicting Bolan's downfall. It was a mellower and fuller sound. It was an angry album too. He was fighting to remain a teenage idol and the crown was slipping — he was dealing in a very unstable genre, so it was just as well that he was taking a more serious view of his writing and trying to move out of pop and into rock.

"I won't stand and be jeered at when I'm doing something that's a craft I've worked at hard for seven years or more. I've never felt so insecure or such pain as I do now because I'm so exposed musically."

The hold on America was loosening. Marc had had the full weight of Warner Bros. pushing him but America couldn't understand the glam-rock movement until two years later when Bowie broke over there. Later Kiss took over where T. Rex could have been. Bolan was ahead of his time — the fate of the innovator.

Marc was growing tired of glam-rock. "I'm just not into that glam-rock crap stuff" and to prove it he wrote 'Shock Rock'. "It was originally called 'Cock Rock' except that the record company wouldn't let me use that name. It's really based on a chorus – 'if you know how to rock you don't have to shock'. I used it against the so called glam-rock, which I appear to be buttoned up with . . . and which I don't necessarily believe in at all. I mean, I believe in music and the clothes I wear, but the attitude I have had since I was 10. So that's what the song is saying – if you can rock it doesn't really matter if you wear pink satin trousers and a feather boa. Glam-rock is sham rock, Elvis Presley was doing it 15 years ago and Hedy Lamarr was doing it too! So was Gloria Swanson!"

He had this go at the critics and in 'Rapids' he also attacked the parents of his fans in an offbeat way: It's a story about a guy being rejected by the daughter's parents, but then it turns out that although the mother doesn't want the daughter to go with the guy, she wouldn't mind going with him herself!

"It's a situation that I find very real. Sometimes when we have kids over the house, very young kids, we get letters from the mums that say 'come to tea' or 'meanwhile, if you want to come while the kids are at school . . .' it's quite raunchy really, but it's an interesting theory. It's about change of attitude. What's good for the kids is good for the parents . . . if you happen to be pretty.

"Of course what we do is sexual. But the sexual atmosphere is a fun thing; very warm, very sensual, very nice. Not something you should take too seriously because if you do, then anything you do on stage degenerates, becomes obscene and disgusting. It's possible to be sexy without being sleazy. It's ironic really, being called a male sex symbol – when I'm prettier than most chicks . . .

"Sure, I often get accused of being a queer, a fag, but I'm not. (Sorry boys.) Actually I find it very easy to be turned on by people, any people, but I just prefer chicks that's all. I've checked out the other scene, I check everything out – but it just doesn't get me off. I know where I'm at sexually because I've worked it all out, which is more than some people do. So when some guy comes up to me and says 'Marc, are you a fag?' nothing happens to me inside. It doesn't concern me or affect me at all.

"I never was one for beer and sandwiches in working men's clubs. None of that 'let's-go-and-have-a-work-out-in-the-gym-lads stuff. I was never one of the boys. Hung around with chicks. Had my first chick at 10. It's like that ludicrous idea that A Real Man Doesn't Cry. Why not? When I'm upset I cry. All it means is that one is sensitive and if other people can't understand, tough luck on them. I wrote some mean songs . . . some street songs, because I've been hanging out in the street."

In June 1973 Marc released 'The Groover' coupled with 'Midnight'. It charted but it seemed to ascend on the backs of his past hits and Marc sensibly declared, "I doubt if I will be putting out any more records with the same sound. 'The Groover' sold a hundred thousand on the first day out. It's my only answer. We still sell the most records in England out of anybody. We sold thirty-nine million records, ten and a half in England in two years. The point being if anyone can name me anyone that has had 7 number ones, 3 number twos and a number 3 all in 18 months, well . . . Has David Bowie had that? I really hope that David can hang out, I really dig his music.

"I dig Glitter too but Gary isn't . . . well, Tennyson . . . I'd like to play on one side of his records. The greatest thing he ever did was to own up to saying it was mindless crap, which was amazing. That's very truthful. He plays body music but I think he underestimates himself. I don't think it's mindless. They've worked out their riff very well, I'd like to see them rock on.

"Regardless of all, England is still my

home. I've spent so many years ligging all over the country, getting on trains with my suitcase and guitar. I couldn't forget that, I could retire tomorrow but that's not what it's all about. If I didn't work I'd freak out. I'd O.D. in two years and be found in the gutter somewhere . . . I'd miss the live gigs, the contact. I know we're the biggest group in the country, I can feel it in the air, I know it on sales.

"Well I didn't want to get sucked into second generation glam-rock. I did that thing for a year and then after the concert at Wembley there was nowhere to go, except Earls Court and that seemed to have been a disaster for everybody. I felt slightly over-exposed in the papers so I thought I'd back off. I figured I could see what was happening. My next thing won't be glam rock. I'm telling you that babe. I don't want to be involved in any of that.

"Don't you think I handled it well? I wasn't sure until today when all these people I have spoken to have said 'Oh aren't you shrewd Marc'. I actually feel more involved with what's happening on the streets. I'm a street punk. I don't want to get too far away. I'm not a star. I'm an anti-star and always was. I'm not anti-establishment, but for me the whole thing got too cheeky. I wore gold suits and that sort of shit for a while but it was a flash. Billy Fury wore them four years before; it wasn't an innovation. I don't put down anyone who is involved in it but once the vision takes over from the music, they're in bad shape."

What endeared Marc to people was his sense of fun – having people on – camping it up or being mach – pulling ideas out of a hat like rabbits then disregarding them as soon as he'd spoken of them. It was this feeling of being manipulated that made some journalists turn against him. His obvious enjoyment of his own sucess could be a bit wearing if you were a struggling journalist or susceptible to professional jealousy.

"I lie a lot you know. I feel that my credibility as a poet allows me to make things up. The only reason I feel that people are prone to be flash and conceited is due to the fact that they lack inner self-confidence. The only thing I'm aware of nowadays is that when I wake up every morning I'm still alive. I'm not so sure about anything else. I don't think one can be, especially if as a musician you look on what you do as being relatively serious.

"What happened was that I lived out the lunacy, worried and got concerned. Certainly there was a period when I was fucked up and probably needed help. But there was nobody there – there never is when you need them. I never thought I'd survive it. I found that the best way is to accept that life is a tightrope in Leon's immortal words and that it is no good trying to plan everything out. I mean I know certain people around who do all that but the one thing I've never been is a pop puppet. I won't be. If I'm going to bomb out I'll bomb out and if I'm going to be a success I'll be successful.

"My fans are the most important thing in my life but they have to dig me for what I am doing . . . I don't and never have, gone out of my way to please them. I stopped playing in Britain because there were so many other things to be done – like taking on America for instance.

"I owe everything to the kids and for that reason I always try and please them in any way I possibly can. They look on me as being a glamorous pop idol and that's what I try and be but understandably there are times when I feel out of my head and physically and mentally worn out. When I get like that I don't want the kids to see me . . .

"You know, even before I entered the music business I quite expected all the fan adulation that I've received over the last few years. Mentally I was prepared for the things that happened before they actually did. I don't have time to think any more 'WOW' I'm Marc Bolan'. I honestly don't know what it's like to Marc Bolan. I believe the ultimate star is the star who makes it just by being himself. Rod Stewart is an example. I mean he really likes football and that kind of thing. I am just as people think I am. I'm all things real to those who dig me.

"Money, you know, I've made a hell of a lot of the stuff, I never think about getting it but I do think about keeping it. I'm a business man but there again I have to be. I employ a lot of people and their livelihoods are upon my shoulders. I never really socialise with other people in the business apart from my own set. I have to exhibit what I feel within my own surroundings and that helps me build up the confidence I need. Nothing is lasting and I don't deliberately go out of my way to plan for the future.

"Bolan is alive today but he may as well

get knocked down by a car tomorrow anyway? I could lose all my money and that doesn't particularly worry me. I wouldn't be happy being penniless – I do like luxuries, but it wouldn't break my heart. I guess my name will live longer than a record. I'm a life-style.

"Everyone else has revamped 'Get It On' and 'Telegram Sam', except T. Rex. Certainly on 'Metal Guru', 'Children Of The Revolution', 'Solid Gold Easy Action' and 'Twentieth Century Boy', the key, the structure, the tempo, are totally different. I've only got one voice so if you think my voice sounds the same on every record you could say the same thing about Mario Lanza. 'Children Of The Revolution' is nothing like 'Solid Gold Easy Action'. One uses strings, the other black chicks. One is slow, the other super fast."

Marc signed guitarist Jack Green to help him on live gigs. It helped Marc to do better solos – he had a fuller live sound now and they toured America, yet again. This time they took three girl singers with them.

One of these girls was American singer – songwriter – producer and northern soul star, Gloria Jones. She was the daughter of an American preacher and had established herself as an extremely talented singer. They became firm friends.

In April the vocals for the 'Zinc Alloy' album were set down in Los Angeles. Half of it was already in the can. Some of it evolved over a long jamming session in Copenhagen during which Marc laid down some amazing guitar passages.

For the rest of 1973 Marc kept a low profile, holidaying in the Bahamas and letting the glam rock bandwagon die out, then, after an exhausting tour of Australasia and Japan Bill Legend left the band. T. Rex were never quite the same again.

Chapter 8

On November 16, 1973 'Truck On (Tyke)' was released, but it only reached number 15. The screamage was over. 'Truck On (Tyke)' was the first single to feature Gloria Jones and over the next year she became a regular contributor on Marc's records, always in the background with Pat Hall but with her strong voice appearing to grow louder.

In January 1974 a new T. Rex did their first tour of Britain in two years and Marc was determined to make it a memorable one. In 1972 they were very loose, but it was good enough for T. Rex just to take the stage, but now they had to attract serious followers and secure the right to remain in the business.

The new T. Rex consisted of Marc, Steve Currie, Mickey Finn, and two new drummers – Davey Lutton and Paul Fenton, two sax players, as well as Pat Hall and Gloria Jones.

At the end of January a solo single was released, 'Whatever Happened To The Teenage Dream', coupled with 'Satisfaction Pony'. It was to be Marc's last hit for nearly a year.

"The idea of the song is whatever happened to the enthusiasm one felt at the age of 12, and why is one's first screw a drag, however good the second one is. The whole song doesn't necessarily apply to me although the verses do. The song is about growing up."

The single was credited to Marc Bolan and T. Rex although he was now actually touring under the name of Zinc Alloy & The Hidden Riders of Tomorrow, a name he had conjured up. He had said he would change his name to Zinc Alloy and wear an aluminium suit if he became successful, but it wasn't until now that he did so, tongue in cheek.

In February the album 'Zinc Alloy' was released to bad reviews and poor sales although it contained some of the best guitar work anyone on the British scene could have done. The production was too overblown and the material suffered from self-indulgence and from being written for the album rather than for its own sake. Unfortunately there was no one to tell him that he was playing at being Marc Bolan rather than being Marc Feld and writing for his real self.

Marc was achieving greater respect among fellow musicians in 1974 but received only scornful, critical public comments about the album and his spreading waistline. He was taking longer holidays and tax exile was now inevitable.

George Tremlett: "A lot of drinking went on. His records stopped selling as well as they had done. And when your records don't sell you don't get television time and when you don't get television you don't get tours. He went through a down period, he drank a lot. I remember there was a gap of six or nine months between me seeing him and seeing him again. His face and body were puffed out,

his clothes were bursting at the seams, he'd changed a great deal . . . he went to seed and looked it. He was holed up in Monte Carlo for a year—for tax reasons."

In March 1974 Marc parted company with producer Tony Visconti over 'musical differences'.

Finally, in June 1974, Track records released the compilation of early outtakes and demos 'Hard On Love' under the new title 'The Beginning of Doves' and a maxi single 'Jasper C. Debussy'.

On July 13th Marc released his own single 'Light of Love'. It reached a new low – barely entering the charts. This time television coverage was having to be fought for – he was no longer a 'must' for 'Top Of The Pops', he had to take his chance with everybody else. But he had an explanation that was true to character.

"It's got to a point now where I'm such a legendary thing that people aren't really sure if I exist, people look at me in disbelief if I get out of a car or something. They almost whisper 'There's Marc Bolan'. There's a definite air of mystique now which wouldn't have been there had I been doing 'Top Of The Pops' every year and putting out 95 records a year, like everyone else seems to be doing at the moment."

One of Marc's greatest assets was his ability to handle the media. Publicist Altham: "Marc was the perfect PR subject, he knew what the media wanted to hear. He knew that if someone said 'Tell us about your millionaire lifestyle, Marc' he'd say, 'Oh yes, you know, the gold Rolls-Royce and the gold boat and the gold house'. He didn't have any of those things of course but he gave them that sense of excitement that people in that area of national newspaper wanted. They wanted a glamorous figure. He never had as much money as people thought he had. It's always a bit like that. Usually money is invested in various areas or it came in very much later

because of publishing and record royalties, these sort of things. Sometimes you don't see money from a million-selling single for about four years. He was a glamorous figure because he played up to it, it was a pose in the same way as Bowie's things were always poses. He'd just as easily go in and charm somebody in an accountant or solicitor's office in a suit and tie as he would dress up in the most flamboyant furs and frills and things and charm the editor of . . . Gay News!

"You couldn't ever influence him. He'd totally made up his mind about what he was going to do before he did it. Whether you said it was fashionable or not didn't matter one iota.

"He'd do an interview with Judy Simons of the Daily Express, who really liked him, and quite genuinely during the course of an interview she'd say, 'Oh, I like your hat' or something and he'd give it to her. It was probably a favourite hat of his and he'd just give it to her. You'd get the situation where he'd be a Walter Mitty man himself. He'd talk himself into a situation. Because in this game if you don't believe in yourself then no one else is going to. So a silver disc immediately became a gold one, a gold one became a platinum one, and a platinum one became a double platinum. He knew that people always wanted something larger-than-life, so he always exaggerated. And sometimes he actually began to believe that himself. The facts got a bit mixed up in his own mind. He started quoting his own sources which were himself quite often. But that was all part of the game – it's only a game anyway. He would tell the most gross stories if it was for a Sunday

paper or a daily paper like the 'Mirror' or the 'Sun', not caring for a moment if it was true because he realised that was what they wanted. If you came to him from a teenage magazine he would tell you just what they wanted, and if the music papers came to him he would happily string them along as well.

"He was always a star, Bowie said that, always a star. He was a very nice man actually. He had a very good memory for personal detail but many people who have a strong artistic streak also have a strong fantasy streak and can lie convincingly. As long as he was speaking to music paper journalists he could get away with it. Fleet Street don't really care, they're only concerned with what sells newspapers. He could fantasise the whole time and I think there was a considerable gap between what was really going on in his mind and what he was trying to convince the world outside."

Marc auditioned the band for Bowie's 'Diamond Dogs' tour, but he held back keyboard player Dino Dines, who used to play with The Beach Boys, and signed him for T. Rex. He also kept on drummer Davey Lutton from the 'Zinc Alloy' tour. Gloria Jones was now featured on Clavinet as well as backing vocals.

In October 1974 he explained that he was cutting out the theatrical effects – he had used Pink Floyd's lighting engineer on the last tour but for 1975 things would be different.

"... I think you should be able to do it simply on the musical value, especially after seeing David (Bowie). I wouldn't want to compete with that kind of thing. He's much more into a theatrical thing than I ever was ... I found that after doing that tour ('Zinc Alloy') practically everyone else in the world started using fog machines and all that shit. I'll probably still do some things like the exploding cabinet and orgy things like whipping my guitar to death."

Chapter 9

Marc spent more and more time away from England for tax reasons. He left Warner Bros. in America and went to Casablanca who released 'Light of Love' in the States. This combined tracks from 'Zinc Alloy' and the new album 'Bolan's Zip Gun' which wasn't released until February 1975.

Prior to the release of the album a new single, 'Zip Gun Boogie' was released at the beginning of February 1975. It didn't even enter the top 30 and the 'Bolan's Zip Gun' album also flopped. It was a bad album – Bolan's worst, and even the faithful felt let down – what had happened? The main reason for this decline was that he wrote most of the album in the studio and consequently did not have time to develop the songs. They sounded good during the session but only 'Till Dawn' and 'Token of My Love' stood out from the mess. "I haven't slipped," he said "not in my chart. I'm still number one. If you go back nine months, I said then, 'Glam rock is dead'. Now a lot of bands are having problems with their image, adjusting to the changes in the world. Fortunately for me, I'm not involved in that any more because I made my statement clear at the time. I started the first teen wave, but I didn't want to get cemented in that environment.

"I've made a heavy point of not making myself too available this year simply because I didn't want to be around. I don't feel the need to any more. My fans understand that. What I'm trying to do is work within the context of a band, being the spearhead but making it a musical experience rather than a theatrical one.

"There were some tracks on the last album that people didn't really grasp the contents of, lyrically. Every time I put down my comments surrealistically the music press tend to say I'm being pretentious. When I make things really simple they say 'Oh it's only bubblegum'. So you've got the choice of the two. I've been lazy. But suddenly I'm into working again. Since the departure of Tony Visconti my music's been much more heavy and rock'n'rolly – I've been freer in the studio, the way I was when I first started..."

At the end of 1974 Marc's marriage to June broke up and he developed a relationship with Gloria.

"We just grew apart, we couldn't relate to each other any more. Plus I was away most of the time. I guess it's very hard being the wife of a rock star 'cos you have to live in the shadow of someone else and well, I'm a lunatic anyway, all artistic people are."

He'd already recorded most of the next album, 'Futuristic Dragon' and was working on a Gloria Jones album after having dropped the sister Pat Hall LP. At this time Mickey Finn left the music business to buy an antique shop in the King's Road.

'Futuristic Dragon' was originally to be released two or three months after 'Bolan's Zip Gun' but it was decided to shelve it until the normal period of a year later. It sounded very different from its predecessor — it was a lusher and fuller sound — there were strings on it and it wasn't so heavy. But only one or two songs stood out. It was patchy, having been made up from the apparent surfeit of songs that Marc felt were too good to can.

In 1975 Marc got himself back together and released the right track from his forthcoming 'Futuristic Dragon' album. 'New York City' was to return our hero to the British screens and radio waves when released in June 1975. It was the perfect single. A really full drum sound, a riff from 'One Inch Rock', and a two-line repeated lyric. Described by its creator as a "boogie mind poem" it rose to number 15 and assured us all that Boley was back.

"I got the idea for the song one day in New York when I saw a woman walking down the street petting a frog she was carrying. You *have* to write a song about something like that."

Gloria, now Marc's common-law wife, was expecting a baby in September. And the prospect of being a father stabilised him. "I'm going to live like a sane human being because I intend to be around for a long time yet. I was living the life that rock stars are supposed to live, particularly in America. I hadn't slept for five days then suddenly I collapsed.

"The doctor said I had been very lucky. It had been a warning. But if I kept living the way I was I would die. I was told to rest for a month and during that month I had plenty of time to think. My troubles had begun when I moved to the States about 18 months ago to let the teeny bop madness die down. When I was in England, I was always working and led a well-adjusted life. After a concert I would go straight to bed exhausted. When I was on tour I was Mister Health. But when I went to America I spent more of the time just doing crazy things. I used to go into the recording studios at two in the afternoon and emerge at five the next morning. I was living on nervous energy, a bit of 'coke' and 'kapers'.

"In the studios I would work with a bottle of something — Scotch or Tequila — at my elbow. It was madness, and it is all finished with now."

When Marc was interviewed with Telly Savalas on the Thames Television 'Today' programme he took over the interview and started to interview Telly! Consequently he was signed up for 13 programmes as an interviewer. "You know me — I never do anything for very long, but I do enjoy interviewing, and I would like to do it for a while, if only to show that chat shows don't have to be boring. But I am not about to become the new David Frost, thank you very much."

But Marc did only a few interviews — Angie Bowie, Keith Moon, John Mayall and Stan Lee the creator of the Marvel comic characters.

He débuted two new songs on the 'Today' programme,— 'London Boys' and

'Funky London Childhood' both from a new project 'The London Opera' that was never completed.

The follow-up to 'New York City' was released in September 1975. 'Dreamy Lady' was coupled with two tracks – the old standard 'Do You Wanna Dance' (the only non-Bolan composition since Gloria's version of 'Dock of the Bay') and was labelled "T. Rex Disco Party". It charted but it wasn't as strong as 'New York City'.

In September 1975 Rolan Seymour Bolan was born. "I delivered him myself. Very expertly, too. This baby's made all the difference to my life," said Marc. "We share the same birth sign, Libra. He looks like me and having delivered Rolan I feel very involved with him. The most important thing is that he has given me a sense of responsibility. Whenever I feel myself getting silly and maybe thinking of slipping into my old ways I just imagine myself dying and Rolan never really having known me. That's a horrible thought. He's really held me together and he hasn't said a word. I'm lazy but he's made me want to work.

"I was nearly over the edge. I'd had five nervous breakdowns and gone crazy about eight times. You couldn't do what I did and still remain sane. I was a near alcoholic for a while and during a six months stay in the south of France I did nothing but sit in the sun and drink brandy all day. I put on two stone. And I was doing my share of drug-taking. Oh yes, I've filled up my nose many times because drinks and drugs are the crutches of the rock world.

"There's nothing more destructive than to be successful in the entertainment industry. It's a killer, no two ways about it. The thing is at 14 or 15 you get your first guitar and start dreaming your dream about becoming the biggest rock star in the world . . . On the way up people are only too pleased to give you advice. But nobody ever tells you what to do after you've made it. That's when the dream can turn into a nightmare, once you've had the first big hit. That's it, everybody knows you. Failure now would be an embarrassment so you've got to keep it up. That's how the pressure starts and the more famous and successful you get, so the pressure gets greater.

"1976 is going to be a clean year for me. I'll be getting my kicks from playing to the kids again for the first time in three years. You could say I've rediscovered my original dream all over again. I might just marry Gloria for Rolan's sake, but I don't think it's very necessary. I've got nothing against marriage for anybody else. It just doesn't seem to suit me. Of course June and I were very much in love when we married, but the real reason we did it was to have a little happening . . . a nice excuse for a piss-up and a slap-up lunch."

The follow-up to 'Dreamy Lady' was scheduled but not pressed. In fact it is unlikely that it was ever recorded.

The single was collectively called 'Christmas Box' and contained 'Telegram Sam' and 'Metal Guru' on the flip side, and that mystery track 'Christmas Bop' on the top side. It was given a works number and even the T. Rex Wax Co. serial number, Marc 12 but it didn't appear. 'London Boys' was released instead in February 1976, as Marc 13. On the flip side was 'Solid Baby', a track from the 'Zip Gun' album, a policy Marc adopted on three of his future singles. He explained about 'London Boys' – a look back at his Mod days. "I never get worried about anything now because to me that was the hard world to live in. I had an obsession with being top Mod. I changed my clothes five times a day . . . ridiculous. It was a time when you daren't turn up at a club dancing last week's dance steps. I had competition then, more than I've had in pop.

"I felt more famous then too. People would sigh with relief when I left the manor for a short time, and when I got rebuffed by a girl in Wimbledon, you

could almost hear the cheers from my rivals. Because I seldom got that treatment. All the girls ended up falling in love with me sooner or later and I had them all. I've no idea how many, it wasn't very important. I never really felt superior, just very, very lucky. Then when I was 15, I wasn't very sure of myself. I wanted to find out so I went with a bloke. It was so that I'd never have to look back and wonder what I'd missed out on. I felt I should try anything once."

Just after the release of 'London Boys' came the nine month old album 'Futuristic Dragon'. But of course Marc had moved on by now and was determined to get back to rock'n'roll. He had his hair dyed with a gold quiff at the front six months ahead of the punks who would change the music business and give Marc a whole new generation of admirers.

His fortunes were to increase with the release of the single 'I Love To Boogie' in June '76. It was coupled with 'Baby Boomerang', the track from 'The Slider' that had a verse of its lyric used in the TV detective series 'Cannon'. Marc explained how 'I Love To Boogie' came about. "I went out and bought about nine rockabilly albums before I went into the studio to make this new record. I bought them because I wanted to get back to the feel of my original music and having been working with Gloria (Jones) for so long I'd gotten out of it a little.

"I didn't know I was going to cut 'I Love To Boogie' because I hadn't even written it before I went in the studio. I wrote it in 10 minutes and would you believe I came up with the lyrics while I was sitting on the toilet.

"What I did was listen to those nine albums and then come up with that type of sound in my head. I've always worked in that way. Take 'Ride a White Swan' for instance – there's a James Burton guitar lick on that stolen from a Ricky Nelson number. Then on 'Hot Love' the middle sounds as if it's straight out of 'Heartbreak Hotel'. Everybody is influenced to a certain degree by other records and what previous artistes have done. I suppose you could say I acknowledge my roots more obviously than certain other people."

Punk was now exploding on the London scene and Marc declared "I'm the originator of punk rock. In America I was always billed as the Cosmic Punk. It's no wonder everybody is getting back to that raw feeling, back to what real rock'n'roll is all about. With the technical tricks some groups are doing with their music they're getting further away from what it was originally all about."

Chapter 10

In September 1976 he released 'Laser Love' coupled with 'Life's An Elevator'. The line-up on 'Elevator' was Marc and Miller Anderson, the replacement for Jack Green as live backing guitarist. It also included ace session men Herbie Flowers (bass) and Tony Newman (drums). Marc kept Dino Dines on organ but he was now helping Gloria in a solo career. The recording was left acoustic and sparse because they simply couldn't think of anything else to put on it. 'Laser Love' was one of those singles put out between two goodies. It flopped, and the lack of airplay didn't help.

Herbie Flowers: "He just phoned up one day from a studio and said 'Hello, this is Marc Bolan here and we're just cutting some new tracks. Would you like to come up'. Meeting him properly was like meeting a little faerie, an elf. He was everything in life like he was on stage. A beautiful guy, no question about that. Everything about him was thoroughly warm. When we went on the road it was just a laugh, a very happy time for us all, wives, kids and everybody. It was just so easy, lovely and magic on stage. I've worked with hundreds of people in the business but he was really the one, head and shoulders above the rest because it was like a proper group. I mean, working with Bowie was OK but it was still a singer outfront . . . Bolan actually played great guitar and moved great – it wasn't a question of being professional, it was a question of it being absolutely right. It was so easy. All good music should just roll off your tongue and it really did. We didn't do a duff performance at any time."

Marc and Gloria recorded a duet of the old Teddy Bears' number 'To Know Him Is To Love Him' and while she finished her solo album 'Vixen', T. Rex went into strict rehearsal for a tour, and in early 1977 recorded a new album. Marc stopped drinking and consciously made an effort to slim.

"Both the albums that I put out after 'Zinc Alloy' were not albums that I put together properly, they were very bitty, because I was going through a very indecisive time. The problem was that I was living in three countries at the same time for tax reasons and wasn't really on top of what I was doing and wasn't really happy with the overall direction. But the new album 'Dandy In The Underworld' I can guarantee will be a top five album . . ."

Indeed the new single 'Soul Of My Suit' débuted on a TV Special 'Rollin' Bolan' in the last half of '76, was a foretaste of things to come. He came on with a new sleek image, his hair cut short with none of those trademark curls, and wearing a black Italian suit with white tie – very Valentino-like.

"Ah yes. Marcos Bolantino. The greatest screen-lover of them all. It could have been me . . . maybe I'll make a

Valentino film myself to show Russell just how it should be done. With my restrained approach it shouldn't cost more than about £20 million."

The next month would see a tour unparalleled in recent years – T. Rex and première new-wave band The Damned.

"It will be my first tour for two and a half years. I have been sitting around waiting for the pop climate to change, for something like punk rock to come along. I consider myself to be an elder statesman of punk, if you like. Under this veneer of brilliantine, and behind this perfect profile lurks a lad who understands what the punk movement is all about. And I think it is what we all need. The glam rock thing was all right for the early seventies, but by 1974 I was just bored. I got involved with drugs – particularly cocaine. And I started to drink a lot. I just didn't particularly want to be a rock star any more. But 1977 will be different.

"With the arrival of the punks there is suddenly more energy in the business. I have stopped using drugs and drinking. I just want to work. This is going to be my year . . . everybody remembers Rudolf Valentino. And I am determined that everybody will remember me."

The album 'Dandy In The Underworld' was released in March 1977 and was the best thing he'd done since 'Electric Warrior'. It was recorded purely as an album and wasn't just a collection of previously recorded tracks, stock-piled over the last six months as 'Zinc', 'Zip Gun' and 'Dragon' appeared to have been. And because of that it was very, very strong.

Marc: ". . . the new album cut very quickly with the new band – I wrote six tracks in the studio and the rest had been around some time. It's a kind of cross between images and hard rock in a way that I've always wanted. It's got this amazing, unique, odd sound. Like 'Electric Warrior' it sounds like a period . . . there's a little magic. Something was happening when we made it.

"I think from now on I'm not going to record for six months at a time. There's no

point in going in the studios all the time. I've changed my whole approach..."

Herbie Flowers: "The Damned actually treated Marc with so much reverence it was beautiful. We'd all get on the coach and there'd be a terrible row but if Marc said 'cut it out lads, I want to be quiet for 10 minutes', they'd all be quiet like a mouse without there being any hard feelings. I remember one particular night we were driving back from Portsmouth about two o'clock in the morning and we stopped at a 'Little Chef'. It was shut and Tony Howard, our manager, said 'Anyone feel like egg and chips?' And we actually knocked the manager and his wife up and said 'Look, we'll give you twenty quid over the top if you give everybody egg, bacon, sausage, chips and beans, cup of tea and bread and butter.' And so there were 40 of us. The crew, fans, wives and kids, and perhaps another 40 fans of Marc's who'd also piled in and we were in there until five in the morning. It was the most gloriously happy thing. A couple of us would get up and do a little cabaret and everybody would muck in and make tea. That was the kind of feeling Marc had."

In May the little track 'Dandy In The Underworld' was released as a single coupled with 'Groove A Little' and a number not on the album 'Tame My Tiger'.

Then came another long overdue break. He was asked to write a monthly column for Record Mirror. They are like time capsules – perfect explanations of summer 1977.

At the beginning of August he got his own half hour television series on Granada, six weekly programmes titled simply 'Marc' which were to be broadcast Wednesday afternoons from August 24th. The programmes featured the best of the new groups – groups like The Boomtown Rats who Marc rightly predicted would be really big.

In his August column for Record Mirror Marc wrote "I'm back on the 'box' (... just regard it as a little bit of early Joan Crawford 'Hooray for Hollywood') ... my own TV series is something I'm really excited about. It happened because Granada's big chief Johnny Hamp wanted someone to host a rock show which would bridge the gap between today and tomorrow and generate a genuine feeling for young people."

That August Marc released 'Celebrate Summer'. "My new T. Rex single has a

very definite New Wave feel about it. If anyone thinks it is deliberate they are quite right."

With only two pre-recorded TV programmes still to be shown and a new album (which still remains unreleased) Marc was rumoured to be negotiating a new deal with RCA.

Just after 5 am on September 16 1977 Marc was travelling home from Morton's Club in his purple mini driven by Gloria when it left the road and crashed into a tree near Barnes Common, South London. Marc was killed instantly. He was 29.

George Tremlett: "He was so many years younger than people like Lennon, who had the education that Marc hadn't had. Lennon was an Art school graduate, so was John Paul Jones and most of Led Zeppelin, 10CC and Queen. And here was Bolan — struggled up from the back streets with his Dad a caretaker in a block of flats, no great educational advantages, fighting tooth and nail and as good as any of them. But he hadn't got the pieces together yet. He was a total educational failure and said so, and yet through 'Warlock Of Love' you could see some ideas developing, there was a considerable figure there. He died very young. There are some artists who take years to develop and he was one of those. It was all coming together, that's what's so sad about it. I think Bolan was going to come back in a big way — a sort of David Bowie level. I'm convinced of it."

Rosalind Russell: "People will get older and have families and he'll become like James Dean. They'll remember him but they won't particularly want to read about him. They will play the records because it's immediate and effortless. They will put him away in a corner of their brain labelled 'dead hero' and will always remember him and quite rightly so because he was a lovely guy. To us he will always be as big a hero as Elvis Presley."

Discography

Singles

SOLO
The Wizard/Beyond The Rising Sun (Decca F12288) Released November 19, 1965.
The Third Degree/San Francisco Poet (Decca F12413) Released June 3, 1966.
Hippy Gumbo/Misfit (Columbia/Parlophone R5539) Released June 1967.

JOHN'S CHILDREN
Desdemona/Remember Thomas A Beckett (Track 604003) Released May 1967.
Midsummer Night's Scene/Sarah Crazy Child (Track 604005) Unreleased.
Come And Play With Me In The Garden/Sarah Crazy Child (Track 604005) Released 1967.
Go Go Girl/Jagged Time Lapse (Track 604010) Released 1967.

TYRANNOSAURUS REX
Debora/Child Star (Regal Zonophone 3008) Released April 1968.
One Inch Rock/Salamanda Palaganda (Regal Zonophone 3011) Released August 1968.
Pewter Suitor/Warlord Of The Royal Crocodiles (Regal Zonophone 3016) Released January 1969.
King Of The Rumbling Spires/Do You Remember? (Regal Zonophone 3022) Released July 1969.
By The Light Of The Magical Moon/Find A Little Wood (Regal Zonophone 3025) Released January 1970.

T. REX
Ride A White Swan/Is It Love, Summertime Blues (Fly BUG 1) Released October 1970.
Hot Love/King Of The Mountain Cometh, Woodland Rock (Fly BUG 6) Released February 1971.
Get It On/There Was A Time, Raw Ramp (Fly BUG 10) Released July 1971.
Jeepster/Life's A Gas (Fly BUG 16) Released November 1971.
Telegram Sam/Baby Strange, Cadillac (T. Rex 101) Released January 1972.
Debora/One Inch Rock, The Woodland Bop, Seal Of Seasons (Echo 102) Released April 1972.
Metal Guru/Lady, Thunderwing (Marc 1) Released May 1972.
Children Of The Revolution/Jitterbug Love, Sunken Rags (Marc 2) Released September 1972.

Solid Gold Easy Action/Born To Boogie (Marc 3) Released December 1972.
Twentieth Century Boy/Free Angel (Marc 4) Released March 1973.
The Groover/Midnight (Marc 5) Released June 1973.
Truck On (Tyke)/Sitting Here (Marc 6) Released November 1973.
Teenage Dream/Satisfaction Pony (Marc 7) Released January 1974.
Jasper C. Debussy/Hippy Gumbo, The Perfumed Garden Of Gulliver Smith (Track 2094013) Released June 1974.
Light Of Love/Explosive Mouth (Marc 8) Released June 1974.
Zip Gun Boogie/Space Boss (Marc 9) Released February 1975.
New York City/Chrome Sitar (Marc 10) Released June 1975.
Dreamy Lady/Do You Wanna Dance? Dock Of The Bay (Marc 11) (EP called "T. Rex Disco Party") Released September 1975.
Hot Love/Get It On (Fly BUG 66) Released 1975.
Christmas Bop/Telegram Sam, Metal Guru (Marc 12) Unreleased.
London Boys/Solid Baby (Marc 13) Released February 1976.
I Love To Boogie/Baby Boomerang (Marc 14) Released June 1976.
Laser Love/Life's An Elevator (Marc 15) Released September 1976.
The Soul Of My Suit/All Alone (Marc 16) Released February 1977.
Dandy In The Underworld/Groove A Little, Tame My Tiger (Marc 17) Released May 1977.
Celebrate Summer/Ride My Wheels (Marc 18) Released August 1977.
Ride A White Swan, Motivator/Jeepster, Demon Queen (Ant 1) (EP called "Bolan's Best Plus One") Released August 1977.

MARC BOLAN AND GLORIA JONES
To Know You Is To Love You/City Port (EMI 2572) Released January 1977.

LBUMS

My People Were Fair And Had Sky In Their Hair, But Now They're Content To Wear Stars On Their Brows (Regal Zonophone SLRZ 1003) Released July 1968. Tracks: 'Hot Rod Momma', 'Scenescof', 'Child Star', 'Strange Orchestra', 'Chateau In Virgina Waters', 'Dwarfish Trumpet Blues', 'Mustang Ford', 'Afghan Woman', 'Knight', 'Graceful Fat Sheba', 'Wielder Of Words', 'Frowning Ataulepa (My Inca Love).

Marc Bolan (vocals/acoustic guitar), Steve Took (backing vocals/percussion). Children's Story read by John Peel and written by Bolan. Front cover by George Underwood. Engineer: Gerald Chevin.

Producer: Tony Visconti.

Prophets, Seers And Sages/The Angels Of The Ages (Regal Zonophone SLRZ 1005) Released October 1968. Tracks: 'Deboraarobed', 'Stacy Grove', 'Wind Quartets', 'Consuela', 'Trelawny Lawn', 'Aznageel The Mage', 'The Friends', 'Salamanda Palaganda', 'Our Wonderful Brown-Skin Man', 'Oh Harley (The Saltimbanques)', 'Eastern Spell', 'The Travelling Tragition', 'Juniper Suction', 'Scenescof Dynasty'.

Produced by Tony Visconti. Engineer: Malcolm Toft. Marc Bolan (vocals/guitars), Steve Took (backing vocals/percussion). Recorded at Trident Studios, London. Cover photo by Peter Sanders.

Unicorn (Regal Zonophone SLRZ 1007). Released May 1969. Tracks: 'Chariots Of Silk', 'Pon A Hill', 'The Seal Of Seasons', 'The Throat Of Winter', 'Cat Black (The Wizards Hat)', 'Stones For Avalon', 'She Was Born To Be My Unicorn', 'Like A White Star Tangled And Far, Tulip That's What You Are', 'Warlord Of The Royal Crocodiles', 'Evenings Of Damask', 'Iscariot', 'Nijinsky Hind', 'The Pilgrims Tale', 'The Misty Coast Of Albany', 'Romany Soup'.

Recorded at Trident Studios, London. Engineers: Rob Cabel and Malcolm Toft. Photographs by Pete Sanders. Children's Story read by John Peel. Marc Bolan (vocals/guitars/organ). Steve Took (backing vocals/percussion/bass/piano). Tony Visconti played piano on 'Cat Black' and produced it.

A Beard Of Stars (SLRZ 1013) Released March 1970. Tracks: 'Prelude', 'A Day Laye', 'The Woodland Bop', 'Fist Heart Mighty Dawn Dart', 'Pavilions of Sun', 'Organ Blues', 'By The Light Of A Magical Moon', 'Wind Cheetah', 'A Beard Of Stars', 'Great Horse', 'Dragons Ear', 'Lofty Skies', 'Love', 'Elemental Child'.

Produced by Tony Visconti. Engineer: Malcolm Toft. Recorded at Trident, London. Cover design by June Child. Photographs by Pete Sanders. Marc Bolan (vocals/lead guitar/organ/bass). Mickey Finn (backing vocals/bass/drums/organ/percussion).

T. Rex (Hi-Fly 2) Released December 1970. Tracks: 'The Children Of Rarn', 'Jewel', 'The Visit', 'Childe', 'The Time Of Love Is Now', 'Diamond Meadows', 'Root Of Star', 'Beltane Walk', 'Is It Love?', 'One Inch Rock', 'Summer Deep', 'Seagull Woman', 'Suneye', 'The Wizard', 'Children Of Rarn' (Reprise).

Marc Bolan (vocals/guitars/bass/organ), Mickey Finn (backing vocals/bass/drums/percussion). Howard Kaylan and Mark Volman (backing vocals). Produced and string arrangements by Tony Visconti. Engineer: Roy Thomas Baker. Cover by Pete Sanders. Recorded at Trident, London.

The Best of T. Rex (Fly Ton 2) Released March 1971. Tracks: 'Debora', 'Child Star', 'Cat Black (The Wizards Hat)', 'Consuela', 'Strange Orchestras', 'Find A Little Wood', 'Once Upon The Seas Of Abyssinia', 'One Inch Rock', 'Salamanda Palaganda', 'Lofty Skies', 'Stacey Grove', 'King Of The Rumbling Spires', 'Blessed Wild Apple Girl', 'Elemental Child'.

Electric Warrior (Fly Hi-Fly 6) Released September 1971. Tracks: 'Mambo Sun', 'Cosmic Dancer', 'Jeepster', 'Monolith', 'Lean Woman Blues', 'Get It On', 'Planet Queen', 'Girl', 'The Motivator', 'Life's A Gas', 'Rip Off'.

Produced by Tony Visconti. String arranger: Visconti. Engineers: Malcolm Cecil, Martin Rushent, Rik Pekkonnen, and Roy Thomas Baker. Cover photo by Spud Murphy from a concept by June Child and designed by Hipgnosis. Inside sleeve drawings by George Underwood. Recorded at Wally Heider (LA), Media Sound (NY), Trident and Advision, London. Marc Bolan (vocals/guitar), Mickey Finn (backing vocals/percussion), Steve Currie (bass), Bill Legend (drums), Ian MacDonald (saxophones), Burt Collins (flugel horn), Howard Kaylan and Mark Volman (backing vocals), and Rick Wakeman (piano).

My People Were Fair/Prophets, Seers And Sages (Fly Too Fa 3/4) Released April 1972.

First two albums re-released as a back to back doublepack.

Bolan Boogie (Hi-Fly 8) Released May 1972. Tracks: 'Get It On', 'Beltane Walk', 'King Of The Mountain Cometh', 'Jewel', 'She Was Born To Be My Unicorn', 'Dove', 'Woodland Rock', 'Ride A White Swan', 'Raw Ramp', 'Jeepster', 'Fist Heart Mighty Dawn Dart', 'By The Light Of A Magical Moon', 'Summertime Blues', 'Hot Love'.

The Slider (BLN 5001) Released July 1972. Tracks: 'Metal Guru', 'Mystic Lady', 'Rock On', 'The Slider', 'Baby Boomerang', 'Spaceball Ricochet', 'Buick Mackane', 'Telegram Sam', 'Rabbit Fighter', 'Baby Strange', 'Ballrooms Of Mars', 'Chariot Choogle', 'Main Man'.

Marc Bolan (vocals/guitars), Mickey Finn (backing vocals/congas/hand percussion), Steve Currie (bass), Bill Legend (drums), Tony Visconti, Howard Kaylan and Mark Volman (backing vocals), David Bowie (backing vocals/sax/acoustic guitar). Orchestra conducted by David Katz. String arrangements by Tony Visconti. Produced by Tony Visconti. Cover by Visconti/Starr. Engineer: Dominique Freddy Hanson. Recorded at Rosenberg Studios, Copenhagen and Chateau D'Herouville, France.

Ride A White Swan (MFP 5274) Released Spring 1972. Budget compilation.

Unicorn/Beard Of Stars doublepack reissue (Fly Toofa 5/6) Released November 1972.

Tanx (BLN 5002) Released March 1973. Tracks: 'Tenement Lady', 'Rapids', 'Mister Mister', 'Broken Hearted Blues', 'Country Honey', 'Electric Slim And The Factory Hen', 'Mad Donna', 'Born To Boogie', 'Life Is Strange', 'The Street And Babe Shadow', 'Highway Knees', 'Left Hand Luke'.

Marc Bolan (vocals and guitars), Mickey Finn (backing vocals/congas), Steve Currie (bass), Bill Legend (drums),

David Bowie (sax), Uncredited 19 year old French piano player. Produced by Tony Visconti. String arrangements by Visconti. Recorded at Chateau D'Herouville, Paris and Rosenberg Studios, Copenhagen. Cover by John Kosh. Pictures by Mike Putland and Pete Howe.

T. Rex Great Hits (BLN 5003) Released September 1973. Tracks: 'Telegram Sam', 'Jitterbug Love', 'Lady', 'Metal Guru', 'Thunderwing', 'Sunken Rags', 'Solid Gold Easy Action', 'Twentieth Century Boy', 'Midnight', 'The Slider', 'Born To Boogie', 'Children Of The Revolution', 'Shock Rock', 'The Groover'.

Zinc Alloy And The Hidden Riders Of Tomorrow (BLNA 7751) Released February 1974. Tracks: 'Venus Loon', 'Sound Pit', 'Explosive Mouth', 'Nameless Wilderness', 'Painless Persuasion V', 'The Meathawk Immaculate', 'The Avengers (Superbad)', 'The Leopards Featuring Gardenia And The Mighty Slug', 'Galaxy', 'Change', 'Liquid Gang', 'Carsmile Smith And The Old One', 'You Got To Jive To Stay Alive', 'Spanish Midnight', 'Interstellar Soul', 'Teenage Dream'.

Marc Bolan (vocals/guitars), Mickey Finn (backing vocals/percussion), Jack Green (rhythm guitar), B. J. Cole (steel guitar), Danny Thompson (cello). Lonnie Jordon (piano), Steve Currie (bass),

Davey Lutton (drums). Backing vocals by Gloria Jones, Big Richard, Pat Hall. Orchestra conducted by David Katz. String arrangements by Tony Visconti. Produced by Marc Bolan and Tony Visconti. Recorded at Electric Ladyland, Los Angeles.

The Beginning Of Doves (Track 2410) Released June 1974. Tracks: 'Jasper C. Debussy', 'Lunacy's Back', 'Beyond The Risin' Sun', 'Black And White Incident', 'Observations', 'Eastern Spell', 'You Got The Power', 'Hippy Gumbo', 'Sara Crazy Child', 'Rings Of Fortune', 'Hot Red Momma', 'The Beginning Of Doves', 'Mustang Ford', 'Pictures Of Purple People', 'One Inch Rock', 'Jasmine '49', 'Charlie', 'Misty Mist', 'Cat Black', 'Sally Was An Angel'.

A compilation of tracks from the early years.

Get It On (Sounds Superb) Budget compilation (SPR 90059) Released December 1974. Tracks: 'Get It On', 'Mambo Sun', 'Planet Queen', 'Rip Off', 'Lean Woman Blues', 'Hot Love', 'Raw Ramp', 'Summertime Blues', 'The Motivator', 'Cosmic Dancer', 'Beltane Walk', 'Ride A White Swan'.

Bolan Zip Gun (BLNA 7752) Released February 1975. Tracks: 'Light Of Love', 'Solid Baby', 'Precious Star', 'Token Of My Love', 'Space Boss', 'Think Zink', 'Till Dawn', 'Girl In The Thunderbolt Suit', 'I Really Love You Babe', 'Golden Belt', 'Zip Gun Boogie'.

Marc Bolan (vocals/guitars), Mickey Finn (hand percussion), Dino Dines (keyboards), Gloria Jones (backing vocals/clavinet), Steve Currie (bass), Harry Niellson (backing vocals), Davey Lutton (drums), David Bowie (sax), Paul Fenton (drums on 'Solid Baby'). Producer: Marc Bolan. Engineer: Gary Ulmer. Recorded at Music Records Inc. Hollywood.

Futuristic Dragon (BLN 5004) Released March 1976. Tracks: 'Intro-Futuristic Dragon', 'Jupiter Liar', 'Chrome Sitar', 'All Alone', 'New York City', 'My Little Baby', 'Calling All Destroyers', 'Theme For A Dragon', 'Sensation Boulevard', 'Ride My Wheels', 'Dreamy Lady', 'Dawn Storm', 'Casual Agent'.

Marc Bolan (vocals/guitar-moog), Gloria Jones (backing vocals/clavinet), Steve Currie (bass), Dino Dines (organ/keyboards), Davey Lutton and Paul Fenton (drums), Tyrone Scott (backing vocals), David Bowie (sax). Strings by Jimmy Haskell. Cover by George Underwood. Engineers: Gary Ulmer, Ray and Mike. Recorded at Music Recorders, Hollywood, USA.

Dandy In The Underworld (BLN 5005) Released March 1977. Tracks: 'Dandy In The Underworld', 'Crimson Moon', 'Universe', 'I'm A Fool For You Girl', 'I Love To Boogie', 'Visions Of Domino', 'Jason B. Sad', 'Groove A Little', 'Soul Of My Suit', 'Hang-ups', 'Pain And Love', 'Teen Riot Structure'.

Marc Bolan (vocals/guitars/bass/maracas/tambourine/percussion), Steve Harley (backing vocals), Alphalpha (backing vocals), Gloria Jones and Colin Jacas (backing vocals), Dino Dines (keyboards), Steve Currie (bass), Tony Newman (drums), Herbie Flowers (bass), Scott Edwards (bass), Paul Humphreys (drums), Davey Lutton (drums), Paul Fenton (drums), Bud Beadle (sax/flute), Chris Mercer (sax), Miller Anderson (second guitar), J. Long (violin), Steve Gregory (flute). Producer: Marc Bolan. Tape ops: John and Neil. Photos by Allan Ballard. Engineer: Mike Stavrou.